What professionals are saying about

Focus Your Business

by

Steven C. Brandt

"Clearly written. Great examples. Easy to read. A terrific guide for people busy building a company."

-Donn Viola, EVP, Mack Trucks

"This is the right book for serious builders of businesses."

-J. Frederick Merz, Jr., CEO, Scott Specialty Gases

"A welcome change from all the single-theme management books. It is a user-friendly mix of practical thinking and academic discipline."

-William P. Rutledge, CEO, Allegheny Teledyne, Inc.

"Brandt's crisp, stimulating book is the best I've seen on the complex subject of managing a growth company."

–Dr. W. Keith Kennedy, CEO, Watkins-Johnson Co.

"*Focus Your Business* is a timely antidote to complexity."

-Dr. Ken Melmon, Director, Immulogic

"*Focus* is excellent. It covers the whole range of positioning issues faced by emerging company management teams."

-Stuart R. Foster, retired CEO, US BANK of California

'Managing a growth company is complicated. Brandt's 'formula' is short on fads and long on fundamentals–a splendid blend of analytics and common sense."

-James M. Osterhoff, CFO, US West

"Brandt weaves sophisticated concepts and real world experience into a very usable prescription for dealing with these times."

-Roger Salquist, CEO, Calgene

D0251667

Focus Your Business:
Strategic Planning in Emerging Companies
by
Steven C. Brandt

Copyright © 1997 by Steven C. Brandt
Parts of this book were included in an earlier book by the author
titled *Strategic Planning In Emerging Companies*.

All rights reserved. No part of this book may be reproduced or
transmitted in any form or by any means, electronic or mechanical,
including photocopying, recording or by any other information storage
and retrieval system without written permission from the author,
except for the inclusion of brief quotations in a review.

Published by:
Archipelago Publishing
P.O. Box 1249
Friday Harbor, WA 98250
(800) 360-6166 Fax: 360-378-7097
info@gmex.com
http://www.gmex.com

Library of Congress Catalog Card Number: 96-85842

ISBN 1-888925-03-5

Book Design & Layout by Art Design, Friday Harbor, WA
Printed in the U.S.A.

FOCUS YOUR BUSINESS

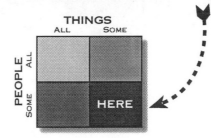

STRATEGIC PLANNING

IN

EMERGING COMPANIES

Archipelago Publishing
Friday Harbor, Washington

P.O. Box 1249, Friday Harbor WA 98250 • 800-360-6166

ABOUT THE AUTHOR

 Steven C. Brandt is an experienced entrepreneur, company president, author, and faculty veteran of 21 years at the Stanford University Graduate School of Business in the heart of Silicon Valley. At Stanford he taught New Enterprises, Business Strategy, and Small Business Management to over 4,000 executives and MBAs during the '70s, '80s, and '90s. He has been a director of three public companies in or near Silicon Valley—a semiconductor company, a solar products company, and a bank. He has also been the cofounder/president of four different businesses in a range of industries including software, educational products, food, and sports services. Brandt has been a direct participant in the development of over twenty other new enterprises involved in everything from sailboats and biotechnology to music and artificial intelligence. The author, who has BSME, MBA, and PhD degrees, has written three other popular business books—*Entrepreneuring in Established Companies, Entrepreneuring: The Ten Commandments for Building a Growth Company,* and *Strategic Planning in Emerging Companies.* He has a new video series entitled, *Managing the Emerging Company.* Today the author lives in a small community where he continues to develop materials for building businesses. Locally he is a hospital district commissioner and a land trust board member.

TABLE OF CONTENTS

*Dedicated
to the home team—
Wooly, Eric & Caprice, and Peter—
and the builders of businesses
around the world.*

Introduction

This book is written to be used. It is about fixing businesses before they break. It is about focusing on just part of the scene even though the whole picture looks great at the moment. It is hard for any of us to ease away from what seems to be working well, but for builders of businesses there is little choice. As the people in growing companies struggle across the swaying bridge that runs from the brink of survival to the land of established competitors, more often than not they are carrying too much baggage. The cumulative weight of initiatives that helped them get to the bridge now is hazardous. The load needs to be lightened. Some things and/or some people (customers) need to be discarded in order to complete the crossing fit for the battles ahead. The process of lightening up is called focusing. Everyone agrees that the enterprise can't be all things to all people. This book is about being some things to some people, about being HERE in the diagram below.

THINGS

	All	Some
All	IMPOSSIBLE!	DIFFICULT
Some	HARD TO DO	HERE!

PEOPLE

Focus Your Business

The nature of emerging companies is that the people therein have many opportunities, sharply limited resources, and a steady breeze of new tasks born of the increasing size and complexity that accompanies business mastery. Such organizations are no longer just eager little companies out of sight of the major players—the industry giants, unions, government agencies, and corporate neighbors prone to pirating able people. Protective shields of anonymity and adrenaline evaporate. Slowly the contents of *Business Week* or *Forbes* or *Fortune* take on more importance than trade magazines, and feature articles in the *Wall Street Journal* assume meaning in the life of the enterprise. But, of course, there is little time to read anything non-operational! The joy of being small and quick are behind, and the benefits of being firmly established are still ahead. The notion of a longer-range plan slips into discussions between key players in a whisper. Company strategy gradually becomes nonacademic in the galaxy of concerns about how best to build the business in the days ahead. Then one day the sun rises on a need to focus or refocus the business in order to get the maximum mileage out of the finite resources available.

Comprehensive strategic planning can help. It involves both questions of what the enterprise is to become and how it will become it. Properly done, it highlights which baggage to discard in order to free up key people and dollars for reinvestment. **A sound plan is usually simple so it can be executed mostly by ordinary people.** A simple plan for an emerging company comes from straightforward thinking by informed builders. The contents of this book reflect my attempt to pull together in a coherent, readable fashion the best both from the real world of actual, current practice and from the practical side of the business academic world.

Strategic planning has come a long way since the early 1980s. In those days it was fairly mechanical and directed primarily to product and market positioning issues. The unspoken assumption was that, given the right product/market choices, the people of a given enterprise could and would make any needed mid-course corrections to pursue the choices, i.e. to execute the plan for the business. In many respects, strategic planning was quite cerebral. It typically revolved around the analysis of things that could be counted, and it was made digestible with the help of bubble charts and other graphic techniques. Today strategic planning has a spotty track record. The corporate carnage of the last decade point up the fact that product/market choices are necessary but insufficient. To be sure, an emerging company needs to have thoughtful product/market choices; but it also needs to have the right people, organization design, and culture, to name a few of the other ingredients of a comprehensive blueprint for the future.

Focus Your Business is organized into fifteen chapters. The first five are familiar toll booths along the swaying bridge. The tolls must be paid to buy the time required to step back from day-to-day pressures to do serious planning. The next six chapters provide the mental mechanics for focusing. The last four are road signs pointing the way to success over the long haul in the land of established competitors.

History shows that being first is not enough in the rambunctious world of business. The list is long of pioneering companies that stormed their markets, grabbed the gold ring, and later dropped it. And the list gets longer day by day. Remember Prodigy when it sat atop the on-line market? Or Apple Computer in the 1980s? Or Ampex with the first video recorders? Or VW with its Beetle and A&W with its roadside hamburger stands? Focus and execution and refocus are required to construct a going concern that lasts as the operating environment evolves.

Focus and execution are the products of solid strategic planning that transcends management fashions. In recent times, reengineering has come and gone, downsizing has bottomed out, and TQM has faded into the background. Savvy people are back to the basics—if they ever left them. They aim to build their companies with a core of informed people enthused about selling distinguishable products and services profitably to selected segments, and they know today the trick is to get bigger without getting fatter.

Much of what is in this book comes from my exposure to people like Mel Cruger, Freeman Ford, Bob Hannah, Woody Howse, Bob Jaedicke, Ray Loen, Forbes Powell, Gary Riley, and Ken Siford. These people and thousands like them have built or are building substantial companies for the long haul. This book is written to serve all such builders.

Steven C. Brandt
Friday Harbor, Washington USA

Preview
Chapters 1-5

The following five chapters offer perspective on why and how builders of growing companies need to adapt their ways—their managing practices—as their companies blossom. With proper perspective, it is easier to make changes before things break. In the highly charged atmosphere of more and more sales volume, it often hard to spend time on the discipline of tightly positioning a company for continuing success beyond the current budget cycle. These chapters can help.

It's actually quite easy to get temporarily excited about focusing your business and strategic planning matters. After all, big-picture thinking *is* fun, and besides, who would vote for being out of focus? But more often than not, good intentions evaporate in the heat of day-to-day pressures. What is expedient drives out what is important. The only antidote to this tendency–and the tendency seems to be particularly acute for entrepreneurial-minded souls–is an understanding that there is a personal price builders must pay when their companies grow in size and complexity. The price is that they must give up some of what worked well for them in the past and replace it with new approaches and fresh thinking.

1
Dimensions
of
Planning

*"The real voyage of discovery consists not in
seeking new landscapes but in having new eyes."*
- Proust

Words are the wheels for ideas, but unfortunately
the language of business is very imprecise. For example,
vision, objectives, strategy, and organization are common
terms which have meanings that vary between
companies and even between individuals within
companies. Fuzzy definitions hamper the formation and
execution of sound plans. One useful by-product of an
effective planning process in a growing enterprise is the
facilitation of communication between members of the
business-building team. Planning provides the
opportunity for people to agree upon a vocabulary unique
to the enterprise.

> **KEY POINT 1: Identify and use a precise
> vocabulary within your company.**

This Key Point applies to the shared experience of
this book, too, wherein the partners—reader and writer—

need parallel definitions for major words. Here are definitions for important words in this book.

Operating Environment: External *and* internal reality which must be dealt with in building a business.

Expectations: End results to be accomplished by the people of the enterprise.

Business Strategy: Summary of what will be sold, to whom, in pursuit of expectations.

Planning: Predetermining a course of action to which resources will be committed.

Strategic Planning: A disciplined, senior form of planning aimed at positioning an enterprise to pursue expectations successfully on a continuing basis.

These five terms constitute a core vocabulary for building a company that lasts.

Levels of Planning. In actual practice there are three levels of planning required in an emerging company with high ambitions. Each level has its own participants, basic time horizons, and tasks, although the different levels often become mingled if not entangled in a fast growing company where most people wear several hats. The table below summarizes the work to be done.

Levels	Main Participants or Process Leaders	Time Horizon	Lead Task
Corporate	Officers	Beyond current budget cycle	Set expectations; Refine biz to be in, not in.
Business	Profit center managers	Current budget cycle	Product/market selection
Functional	Department teams	Operating deadlines	Allocating resources

Levels of Planning

KEY POINT 2: Consciously separate the different levels of planning.

Key Point 2 is particularly important. Sometimes confusion is spawned by rapid expansion. For example, it is not unusual to find people in R&D, central marketing, and various profit centers simultaneously pulling in different directions. The stress on the system is compounded further when the profit center chiefs and the head of R&D are also corporate officers responsible for the health of the total enterprise! The emerging company that is still a single profit center faces a special challenge in that the corporate and business levels of planning essentially merge. This makes it even harder for the senior people to look up from the grindstone of short-term operations–today's business–and out along the road ahead for answers to the questions in the planning diamond.

Planning Diamond. At all three planning levels, the basic issues are the same. They are shown below. The answers to the questions at any particular level provide input for planning at the adjoining level(s).

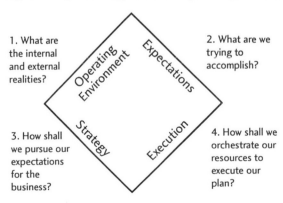

1. What are the internal and external realities?

Operating Environment

Expectations

2. What are we trying to accomplish?

3. How shall we pursue our expectations for the business?

Strategy

Execution

4. How shall we orchestrate our resources to execute our plan?

Planning Diamond

Why all the fuss about language and levels? There is a class of companies that occupy the space below the Fortune 500-size companies. Companies in this class are often directed by people with big ambitions and a shortage of cash, time, and staff. Yet from this class will emerge tomorrow's leaders. Some companies happen onto leadership status because of an unexpected technological breakthrough or a windfall generated by others—the government, an inept competitor, or even major customers who do well. Other companies successfully emerge because the key people systematically define and exploit opportunities. They *cause* desired things to happen. They are focused, and they focus their businesses, the heartbeat of this book. Most of the time, such people seem to land on their feet despite oscillations in the economy, radical swings in buying habits, and the increasing pressure that goes with winning. How does this happen? The answer is deceptively simple. *Such builders of businesses grow and change as their enterprises increase in size and complexity.* They recognize that what worked well at $50 million may not work well at $100 million. They have perspective on the changing nature of their jobs.

KEY POINT 3: **Increase the proportion of energy devoted to planning as your enterprise grows in size and/or complexity.**

Take a look at the diagram at the top of the next page, Sales Volume Cutoff for Fortune 500. It shows the sales required to be included in the Fortune 500 over the past forty years. In 1955, a company with $50 million in sales was in the Fortune 500, a full-fledged member. In 1995, the smallest company in the Fortune had $2.5 billion in sales! That's *billion.*

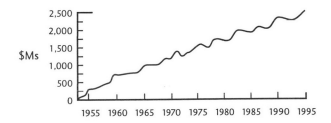

Sales Volume Cutoff for Fortune 500

The construction team of the number 500 company in the mid-1950s had $50 million worth of complexity to manage *and* a strong competitive position, perhaps even the dominant one. In the 1990s, the leadership of a company at even $500 million in sales has $500 million worth of complexity (people, products, markets, and so on) to manage plus plenty of nonmarket subjects to consider. And in many industries, it is unlikely that the $500 million company is the dominant attraction—for customers, talent, financing, or anything else. The game has changed. Today relative smallness alone puts a premium on smartness on the part of builders who want to move their emerging companies up through the pack. To paraphrase a famous Peter Drucker quotation:

Management must increasingly be both effective and efficient. Effective means it does the right things; efficient means it does things right.

Focus is required to do *just* the right things. Strategic planning is the path to get from here to there.

Stages of Company Growth. There is another element of perspective basic to this book. In recent years, scholars have analyzed many, many companies in an effort to discern any distinct and recurring patterns or stages through which companies typically pass. Most notable among these efforts was a comprehensive study by Professor Larry E. Greiner of USC. The conclusion reached by Greiner and other researchers is that, indeed, there are common stages and crisis points, and that an appreciation of them can assist people in piloting their enterprises through time. The most important stages in the corporate metamorphosis are illustrated in the diagram below.[1] (All references are listed on page 167.)

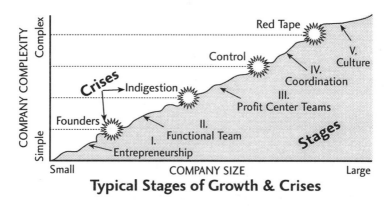

Typical Stages of Growth & Crises

As companies become larger (x-axis), they usually become more complex (y-axis), too, due to product line or market expansion, or both. (More on this in Chapter 4.) As a company becomes more complex, the managing practices used by key people usually need to change, for example, often the organization needs to be redesigned. Growth Stage I in the diagram, **Entrepreneurship**, illustrates this phenomenon. One person or a small team with an idea works hard, informally, and quickly to launch a simple, new enterprise. A high percentage of start-ups succeed for a while *because* of the energy (sweat equity) applied, but the survival-minded dedication of the start-up team often also contains the seeds for the first well-known crisis, the **Founders** crisis. The entrepreneurs try to do everything themselves; they will not take their hands off the wheel for even a moment. The company's needs—spawned by growth—exceed the grasp of the one or two individuals in the driver's seat. The fledgling enterprise hits speed bumps and skids off the road to success, *because* of success. It happens every day.

What does it take to stay on the road and move into the typical Stage II of growth? Usually it takes the addition of talent in order to achieve a full, well-rounded **Functional Team**. Such a team might include accounting or manufacturing or marketing or financing expertise, depending on the needs of the business and the voids in the founding-team's repertoire. In this second stage an entrepreneur, if he or she is to make the transition, must begin getting results *through others*, as opposed to through his or her own individual effort. Many entrepreneurs find this a tough transition to make, and many don't make it. Their companies, then, peak or bow out at the first crisis. Once again, it happens every day.

In companies where the Founders crisis is cleared, progress along the growth road can continue. In Stage II, systematic planning becomes more important as additional products and markets are evaluated. Resource allocation shows up as a regular agenda item since there are often more opportunities than cash and people to cover them. Given smart decisions by a qualified and informed functional team, the business continues to emerge in Stage II. It often also becomes rapidly more complex. This is the perfect condition for the second common crisis, **Indigestion**. The single layer of general management normally found in an organization designed around functions simply can no longer efficiently handle the diverse issues, problems, and questions flooding in from the various functional chiefs. The general management gets overloaded. Across the company symptoms start to appear: deadlines are missed, budgets are exceeded, communications bog down, silly mistakes are made. The quality of decisions declines because everyone is so busy and the senior people have started losing contact with the realities at the customer interface. For a second time, the enterprise is paying the price of growth, namely a crisis that signals big-time change is required (to keep on succeeding). The best medicine is often to break the company into smaller, more manageable pieces–to decentralize into **Profit Center Teams**.

Stage III growth, with its multiple profit centers, means that at least one additional layer of general management is added to the organization design. On paper at least, this pushes some key decisions back down closer to the customer base. Profit centers are typically formed around either various product lines (e.g. A, B, C), pieces of geography (East, West), or types of customer (Retail, OEM). The intention is that each profit center management team will deal with a fairly homogeneous range of issues. Decentralization is one way of encouraging "focus" at the operating level. Done properly, it can make a growing company more nimble. Stage III growth, however, like the other stages, carries with it the seeds of another crisis. The actions of relatively independent profit centers may well breed internal competition as well as a crisis of **Control**.

Profit center managers have a tendency to go in different directions in search of growth. When this happens, the total enterprise, at best, becomes merely the sum of the operating parts instead of more than the sum. This is not necessarily bad news, but it is not unusual for senior business builders at the center of things to get increasingly uneasy. They sense they are losing touch with what is going on, and often they are because more and more they are managing essentially by remote control. The overall direction of the enterprise becomes unclear, perhaps even confusing, as it stretches in various directions. There is a loss of control in the sense that key people lack an intimate grasp of what is going on across the enterprise. Conglomerates are the ultimate expression of this condition. They usually have little center, core, or focus.

The antidote is **Coordination**, Stage IV. The objective is cooperation and synergism among divisions to exploit competitive advantages jointly. Coordination usually requires added management information systems, reporting mechanisms, and an expanded planning and performance review schedule. In short, the people in the company get involved in more meetings, manuals, and memos throughout the year.

These initiatives may, in time, bring about a higher degree of cooperation and more focus. Experience indicates they also often usher in the next crisis, **Red Tape**. Busy business builders in the operating units of the emerging company find they must spend two-thirds of their time justifying what they do with the remaining third. Bureaucracy is at hand.

How can the red tape be cut (or avoided) without having the pieces of the emerging enterprise diverge so far that the company becomes a blur? Companies have tried a variety of human overrides to numbers-dominated control systems. These include task forces, matrix structures, interdivisional committees, and various administrative maneuvers designed to promote the productive interaction of seasoned people for the good of the whole organization. These overrides are occasionally successful. But the most enduring way to accomplish (or retain) an optimal singleness-of-purpose in an emerging company is to emphasize and cultivate a deep, clearly defined corporate **Culture**, Stage IV in the diagram. Rather than trying to impose order or cooperation across an otherwise unruly company via external processes, an attempt is made to *internalize* desired behavior—at least in the key players throughout the growing company. Put another way, a culture is an alternative to command and control processes for encouraging people to do things. As a practical matter, both processes and culture are key managing variables, major tools in a business builder's tool box. All (eight) of the variables need be thought about strategically. (More on this in Chapter 15.) The best time to define and consciously begin culti-vating a culture is when a company is still young and pliable–say in Stages I and II. Every emerging company ends up with a culture of one kind or another, but, un-planned, it may be inconsistent with other important variables.

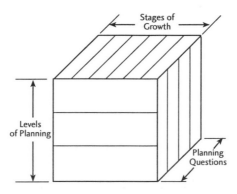

Dimensions of Planning

In summary, there are three important dimensions of planning. The three form a framework for thinking about what an emerging company is to become and how it will become it, about getting a business into focus and carrying out plans made. These dimensions are illus-trated in the diagram above. With an awareness of the different levels, the questions, and the typical stages of growth through which most successful companies pass, the issue of how to keep on succeeding can be addressed systematically by builders of businesses and the people with whom they work.

2
Managing By Objectives

"Far better it is to dare mighty things..."
- Teddy Roosevelt

To dare mighty things is to set expectations. Legions of experts past and present agree that the greatest single mark of leadership is the ability to bring people to unexpected levels of achievement. It is human nature to stretch, to build, to reach, to work toward legitimate accomplishments–personal and community, including one's work community. An underlying theme for this book is that *people tend to rise to meet expectations.* A major requirement of effective strategic planning is that it should be done within a framework of expectations for the enterprise. Otherwise, planning is a purposeless exercise.

In a business setting, expectations may be expressed in terms having different degrees of abstraction. As a practical matter, they can exist at any one of three levels of what can usefully be called the Expectations Pyramid.

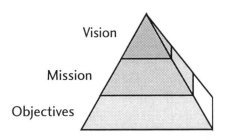

Expectations Pyramid

At the top, the apex, is **Vision,** the most abstract level of expectations. A vision can be a driving force, a centerline of purpose for an enterprise. In the mid-1990s, the *Wall Street Journal* carried a front page article with a headline, "AT&T is the Information Superhighway." The article went on to say how the idea was "galvanizing the people of AT&T and surprising the veterans there with its clarity and simplicity at a time when the telecommunications industry is in turmoil." There is a lot of hype connected with visions, but the fact remains they have made and do make a difference in some emerging companies. They can *inspire* and, therefore, affect behavior. Chapter 12 covers visions in more detail.

In the middle of the pyramid is **Mission**. Missions are less abstract, more specific, and typically longer than vision statements. In many respects, effective missions *educate*. They come with different labels. The Hewlett-Packard mission is called the *H-P Way*. At Johnson & Johnson, they have a *Credo*. Elsewhere labels such as *Constitution*, *Principles*, and *Motto* have been used with success. Like visions, missions are a form of expectations. Like visions, missions will be covered in more detail in Chapter 12.

Objectives form the base of the expectations pyramid. They are the subject of this chapter. Objectives are the individual building blocks supporting the pursuit of the mission and vision. Objectives, or goals or targets if you prefer, identify what is to be accomplished this week, this quarter, this year. One of the most well known statements of an objective was made on May 25, 1961 when then President, John F. Kennedy, said: "...that this Nation should commit itself to achieving the goal, before this decade is out, of landing a man on the moon and returning him safely to earth." Objectives–measurable, dated, end results to be achieved–are the minimum form of expectations required to focus your business. Managing by objectives (MBO) is part and parcel of strategic planning in an emerging company.

With the possible exception of human relations, no managing practice has received more attention and publicity than MBO. Since the concept was introduced into the world of business in the early 1960s, there has been a steady stream of books, seminars, videos, and college courses extolling its virtues. Builders of businesses (and not-for-profit enterprises as well) have picked up and legitimized MBO as a practical frame of reference for resource allocation and scheduling. Looking ahead is better for planning than looking back, i.e. extrapolating the past. There are some horror stories, of course, and there is always the question of managing by whose objectives– employee's, stockholder's, or society's. But by and large, business-building teams which select "stretch" targets for themselves and their organizations are more likely to hit them than teams which operate without targets or by gazing into the rearview mirror. Objectives are an expression of expectations.

> **KEY POINT 4: Structure expectations throughout your organization.**

The evidence is overwhelming on this point: Whether the task is to sell more, spend less, serve customers better, or generate new ideas, "in the long run, people hit what they aim at..." to paraphrase Henry David Thoreau. MBO is a discipline that starts with the identification and articulation of the results to be achieved. Making hard choices is the antithesis of going with the flow. The use of objectives requires decisions. Consider the alternatives to MBO.

MBE

MANAGING BY EXTRAPOLATION

Users of this system keep on doing what they have always done. More is normally merrier, and over time, all the graphs in the planning documents have lines that creep upward and to the right. MBE, essentially a historical approach to the future, was adequate during the first half of this century. Then there was a latent, developing-country demand for products and services as the population in the USA grew and shifted from being rural to being more urban. There were also two world wars to fuel consumption. Car companies and their suppliers produced and distributed cars, appliance companies made appliances, banks handled money, and so forth.

Up through the 1950's business was in a relatively steady state in which tomorrow was shaped a lot like yesterday, and the primary task for company builders was to do the same things over and over again with incremental improvements. A look at the national productivity curve during this period shows that, in general, business people succeeded in doing things right, i.e. more efficiently. America supplied much of the world. Business was good.

MBC

MANAGING BY CRISIS

This system, long the specialty of the entrepreneur, has picked up a larger following in recent times for two reasons. First, as outlined in Chapter 1, business life is more complex than it used to be. So there is a steady stream of crises to be handled—enough, in fact, to occupy everyone pretty much full time if they are willing. Second, there are a great many more engineers and technically-oriented people in positions of management responsibility today, and as a group such people tend to be great problem solvers. Give such a person a crisis and he or she will smother it with energy and innovation. And should a gap in the flow of problems to solve occur, chances are good that a crisis can be invented—something nice and tangible. No abstractions, please! In many respects, reengineering of recent fame was a solution in search of sponsors. Unlike many more strategic matters, it was nuts & bolts, a 2H-pencil kind of challenge. MBC is popular. At the end of any given day no one can say the boss didn't earn her or his pay.

MBS

MANAGING BY SUBJECTIVES

As the cat said to Alice when she hesitated along the path to Wonderland, "...if you don't know where you are going, any road will take you there." It is easy for the people in a fast growing company to not know where they are going. Signposts and landmarks pass quickly. Many individuals do the best they can do to get done what they think should be done, but the net impact from everyone may be zero or negative. MBS is dangerous in an emerging company. There are enough threats to the enterprise from outside without confusion inside.

A dictionary definition of the word "subjective" is:

> ...*existing or originating within the observer's mind or sense organ and, hence, incapable of being checked externally or being verified by other persons.*

When directions are weak or mixed or both, MBS results and people are cast adrift: "...any road will take you there." MBS *may* be adequate for a short while when a business is relatively small and simple. If a young enterprise gets off to a good start, momentum can cover a lot of sins and false starts by people groping down blind alleys. However, at some point confusion becomes epidemic. MBS must be abandoned. Otherwise, there will be no answers to the questions sharp people ask: Where are we headed? How are we doing? How am I doing? Emerging company builders unable to provide reasonable answers to such questions are unlikely to attract and/or hold the caliber of talent required to capitalize on a competitive advantage. Few enterprises do more than one thing really well. A focused business has a rallying point—but people need to know what it is.

MBH

MANAGING BY HOPE

Many readers know from personal experience that the pace of living in the business world has increased markedly in recent years. Every business decision these days—staffing, capital investments, new services, etc.—seems to have more strings attached than in earlier times. Certainties are hard to find. And the resulting uncertainties of the times have led more than one team into willy-nilly diversification in the *hope* that going in multiple directions at once will work out. The same uncertainties have seduced other business-building teams into paralysis by analysis in the vain *hope* something will turn up to point the way for the enterprise. MBH is essentially a form of reacting rather than acting, of letting events dictate the action agenda rather than vice versa. It is the other end of the spectrum from MBO. As this book is written, at the behest of Wall Street, hundreds of larger companies are turning from downsizing to sales growth in search of profitability. According to the *WSJ*, evidence of MBH is already piling up!

Airborne Express has tried to grow by cutting prices only to ignite price wars. Unisys Corp. has tried to reposition itself in faster-growing industries only to find competition intense and profits elusive. Nabisco has tried to extend core products only to be hurt by the cost of creating too many variations and cannibalizing their own sales. And Abar Ipsen has tried globalization only to learn that cracking foreign markets is tough. [2]

Establishing measurable, dated objectives in vital areas is a step necessary to useful strategy formulation. For example, one of the major electronics companies in California's Silicon Valley has an explicit corporate objective to maintain a steady level of employment for its people. This objective alongside more traditional financial ones has had and will continue to have an impact on decisions concerning new products, plant locations, and promotion policies. Hewlett-Packard, a company that has successfully emerged over the past twenty years, has long had a corporate objective to grow at a rate consistent with the availability of internally-generated funds. This objective has influenced dividend policy, R&D direction, and marketing strategy including pricing. In short, a strong case can be made for investing whatever time it takes to hammer out and get agreement on objectives, the building blocks of the enterprise.

Objectives can be developed in three categories. They are shown in the diagram, Corporate Objectives.

Corporate Objectives

Financial Performance

Under this heading are the traditional operating-statement measures such as sales growth and profitability as well as balance sheet measures such as return on investment (ROI) and inventory turns. For example, the fabled "DuPont formula" captures in a comprehensive way how an organization is performing financially:

ROE = ROS x Asset Turns x Leverage

Return on Equity =s Return on Sales x Asset Turns x Debt/Equity ratio.

Market Performance

This category contains measures such as the relative position in the marketplace, new product revenues, innovation indicators such as new patents applied for, and customer satisfaction indexes. Interest in market-place performance measures has grown more intense in recent years in the wake of global competition and a great deal of press on the positive benefits of being a leader in your chosen business. "You gotta be #1, 2, or 3...or you're outta GE," is the chant at General Electric. Since the early 1980s, CEO Jack Welch has focused the operating units of GE on staying at or getting to the top of the leadership pole in their respective industries. "The more people use your product, the more advantage you have—

or, to put it another way, the bigger your installed base, the better off you are," says W. Brian Authur, an economist at both Stanford and the Sante Fe Institute. [3] There is more on marketplace performance ahead in Chapter 8.

Nonmarket Performance

This is the toughest category for several reasons. First, there are citizenship questions. Does a business exist to serve society, customers, shareholders, employees, or some esoteric mix of these various constituencies? Does the bottom line justify anything and everything, or is it just one yardstick among several? In an increasingly wired world, what obligations, if any, does a business enterprise have to go beyond the letter of the law? For example, to what extent is an Internet company a citizen with citizenship obligations? Should such a company have nonmarket objectives? These questions are alive today. For example, they are regularly raised by candidates for certain public offices.

Second, there are competitive questions. Many nonmarket factors affect the ongoing financial and market performance of a company. For example, government regulation and deregulation help and hamper different firms; so do the efforts of activist groups, the media, the Federal Reserve, and school systems which educate entrants to the work force. David Baron of the Stanford Graduate School of Business puts it well in his award-winning article, Integrated Strategy:

The nonmarket environment consists of the social, political, and legal arrangements that structure the firm's interactions outside of, and in conjunction with, markets. The nonmarket environment is characterized by four I's: issues, institutions, interests, and information. Issues are what nonmarket strategies address. For example, revision of the Modified Final Judgment that settled the federal antitrust suit against AT&T is a nonmarket issue. The relevant set of institutions for telecommunications issues are the Federal Communications Commission, Congress and its committees, state regulatory commissions, and the federal courts. Interests are individuals and groups with preferences about, or a stake in, an issue. In the case of telecommunications policy, the interests include telecommunications companies, cable companies, media organizations, equipment manufacturers, and consumer and activist groups. Information pertains to what the interested parties know or believe about the relation between actions and consequences and about the preferences and capabilities of the interested parties. In the case of telecommunications policy, information pertains primarily to the likely consequences of deregulation alternatives.[4]

Emerging-company management teams fresh from survival school typically do not have nonmarket issues high on their agendas. Yet it is clear that subjects such as employment, trade policy, the environment, ethical behavior, interest rates, and harassment-free working conditions are all part of the operating environment. As Professor Baron summarizes it: "The principle focus of the strategy formulation process is on the market environment and competitive strategy, but for many firms the nonmarket component can be just as crucial."[4]

So, corporate objectives come in three categories. **Who in an emerging company should be involved in setting the objectives of the enterprise?** Ideally, everyone should be, from company directors to employees–everyone who will play a part in reaching the objectives. Strategy today is less and less the prerogative of the senior people. Nor does it need to be. The business that excels in these supercharged times will be the one that attracts and holds talented, motivated people at all levels, including the board. Such people have alternatives—other places to live, work, and develop social roots and networks. It is unlikely that an emerging enterprise can successfully extend its track record without seriously cultivating its human resources as one of the results to be achieved. "None of us is as smart as all of us," says Philip Condit, the seventh man to run Boeing, the world's largest aircraft manufacturer. As Forbes magazine put it: "Booming on the surface, Boeing is in fact a company in transition." [5] That is, it is emerging!

Regular boss/subordinate interchange on setting objectives and evaluating performance in accomplishing them can provide the central nervous system for a high-growth company. MBO, the systematic use of objectives, may well be the single most important management practice for keeping a company together and on track. Objectives are the pumping heart of structured expectations. Bob Noyce, cofounder of Intel, put the issue this way:

I think there's a lot of lip service given to MBO, and it's not practiced. But here everybody writes down what they are going to do and reviews how they did it, how they did against those objectives, not to management, but to the peer group and management. So that's also a communication mechanism between various groups, various divisions, et cetera. [6]

Objectives are a bedrock issue at Intel, a core element of the company's culture. Intel's revenues were over $16 billion in 1995. The company's market position is clearly number one in its industry. And the total return to its shareholders for the ten years between 1985 and 1995 was 118%. In the same ten years, Intel had the greatest growth in earnings per share of all the companies listed in the *Fortune* 500. The complete article describing Noyce's point of view on MBO is included as

Reading I in the back of this book.

Given these thoughts on who should be involved in MBO, how does a willing team proceed? Objective formulation should be the kickoff point for a strategic planning process. This sequencing does not preclude iteration at later steps. Here is a short case study.

> The key builders of a company in Chicago decided somewhat arbitrarily that they would like to achieve a compound sales growth rate of 40% over the coming three years. Subsequent analysis and due consideration of alternative strategies for meeting this acknowledged, ambitious figure revealed that the figure simply could not be met without a major acquisition. A decision was reached to lower the objective to a more conservative 25%, a level at which the company could continue concentrating on building its existing operations—on doing what its senior team knew it could do. The use of an objective along with honest "due consideration" helped this ambitious team recognize and deal with reality.

As an aside, business history books are full of horror stories about big acquisitions seemingly made to reach growth objectives. Close analysis reveals that many large acquisitions of the past twenty years were actually ends in themselves, not means to an end.

There are many benchmarks for setting **financial objectives** including industry sources, competitors, stock market statistics, and bankers. The management of Boise Cascade directed a dramatic turnaround in the company's fortunes after the company nearly went bankrupt some years ago. Near the start of the comeback, the planning team decided that the primary financial indicator of success would henceforth be the return on equity (ROE) of Boise as compared to the ROE of a set of major competitors in the forest products industry. ROE was chosen, according to Cliff Morton, the Vice-President of Corporate Planning at the time, "in order to put management on the same footing as the stockholders." The strategic planning process and the incentive system were keyed to the ROE criterion. At the start of the turnaround effort Boise Cascade's ROE was 3.5%; its selected set of competitors averaged 10.1%. Four year's later Boise achieved 10.7%; its competitors averaged 14.9%. In three more years Boise reached 15.7%; its competitors averaged 16.5% The ROE gap was nearly eliminated. During the same period Boise's stock price rose from $8 to $35 reflecting the vastly improved financial performance of the company. Morton said, "establishing a believable financial goal line was the critical first step."

Market objectives, particularly share of market, came into vogue after a great deal of solid research initiated at GE. The research showed a high correlation between market share and ROI across a wide, cross section of American businesses. The findings led quickly to the nostrum that "If you can't be number one or number two in a specific market, you had best consider getting out," a *Wall Street Journal* front page headline at the time. The research did indicate clearly that the more a company does of something, the better it *should* get at doing it. Note that getting better was not automatic! The bottom line was, and is, that the company best at doing something vis-a-vis its competitors should have the lowest cost structure and, therefore, the highest margins. Pretty simple! It is technically known as the experience-curve phenomenon. It is one of the most powerful and compelling arguments for focusing your business: A company doing the most of some one thing has a start on a favored competitive position. Therefore, market share leadership is often a worthy objective.

Making market share the *primary* objective is not necessarily the wise thing to do in emerging companies.

An all-out campaign for market share fueled by a skimpy cash flow can be fatal! Share has its applications and limitations. Other factors to be weighed are covered in the next chapter. Since most emerging companies do not occupy a dominant position vis-a-vis their competition, selecting any market-performance objectives must be done with care, including a healthy dose of realism.

Nonmarket objectives are the hardest to take seriously and nail down in an emerging company. "Let the big guys worry about such things," is often the attitude. But nonmarket factors are a fact of life. Business builders who systematically address them sooner will be ahead of their competitors who address them later. Nonmarket opportunities and threats need to be boosted to an equal footing with financial and market concerns. In a sense, what Peter Drucker calls "The Network Society" is a reflection of the impact of nonmarket forces on enterprises of all sizes:

The Internet, privatization of major industries in countries around the world, the globalization of money, trade contests between major countries, social trends affecting the work force, the list of noncontrollables is long and seems to be growing. Together they provide the air companies breathe. They cannot be ignored as plans are made.[7]

In summary, managing with objectives is part of selecting desired things to make happen in a busy, shrinking world. Objectives are the threshold to planning in order to focus your business.

3
Excel
at
One Thing

*"We can do anything, but we
can't do everything."*
- Author unknown

"Build a better mousetrap and the world will beat a
path to your door." This phrase is an integral part of
business folklore. "Better" is the key word; it says people
in business are engaged in a competitive vocation. If a
given product or service or enterprise is better, then
another product or service or enterprise is worse. It is
relative position vis-a-vis competition that counts. More
than one emerging company has risen into the limelight
primarily because its competition was weak in one or
more important ways. Such luck usually doesn't last. As
a company   emerges, the level of play escalates.
Recognition of this fact is one reason why the systematic
development of information about competitors is an
important part of strategic planning. Such information
can help you focus your business, help you "Hit 'em where
they ain't," as Dizzy Dean put it.

Better also implies that in what you sell there is incremental value *for the ultimate users*, not for your R&D department, sales force, or controller. More than one emerging company has fallen from grace because its leaders couldn't break the lock the company's engineers or scientists had on product development. It is the world– not your employees or business associates or stockholders–that must crowd the path to your door! When an enterprise has products or services with noticably superior values *and* desired customers are partial to those values, the enterprise has a competitive advantage. Many emerging companies have such an advantage for a while but allow it to wither. Other companies resist changing their approach as their industry matures. One task in building a company for the long haul is that of crafting, or re-crafting, a *sustainable* competitive advantage. Such advantage typically takes one of three basic forms that constitute the Competitive Triangle. Part of the science and art of focusing your business in pursuit of your expectations is to pick one of the three forms in which to excel. Just one.

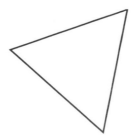

Competitive Triangle

PRODUCT SUPERIORITY

A superior mousetrap might be one that consistently catches more mice because it has a low-noise snap (due to spring design), or because it has cleverly deceptive

visual characteristics (due to graphics design). Such a
trap has a strong chance of doing well in certain dis-
criminating segments of the pest control marketplace if
the trap's virtues are adequately communicated to potential buyers.

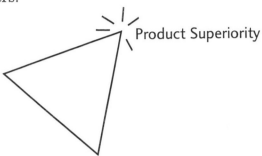

Product Superiority

Product superiority has been and is the primary
method of competing for many manufacturing companies
in the emerging class. Working near the state-of-the-art
is generally important in high-tech companies with a pen-
chant for pushing performance boundaries. Achieving superiority on a continuing basis is no small task, however;
at a minimum, it requires the *commitment of the whole
company!* In effect, the builders must bet the enterprise
on being able to keep coming up with what is new. What
companies come to mind when you think of a continuing
flow of products with unique features and/or performance? How about Intel? Nike? Sony? Timex? Disney?

What does it take to excel in product superiority as
you build your business? It takes product superiority
people, systems, managing style, organization design,
culture, expectations, and financial where-with-all. It
takes the whole works along with discipline and commitment to the point of evangelical fervor! A decision to
base the future of your enterprise on state-of-the-art
product leadership is nontrivial. Whether done in the
lab, in the market place, or both, the search for fresh
ideas is likely to be futile if it is done faintheartedly, or

on a stop/start basis. The fundamental activities needed to produce meaningful innovation require a critical mass of dedicated, appropriately managed talent. That's why it is almost impossible to truly excel in more than one thing.

APPLICATION EXPERTISE

A different critical mass is required for the second way to excel enroute to a sustainable competitive advantage.

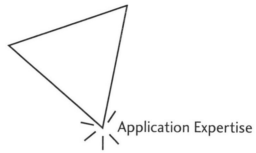

Application Expertise

A product line of mousetraps supported by service that assists buyers with both trap selection and placement will often be worth a premium price to part of the universe of people with mice problems. Many might even "walk a mile" out of the way to purchase such a package. How do builders construct and compete on a reputation for application know-how? Product specifications, design, and engineering usually play a part, of course. So does production expertise including the management of quality and delivery. Installation and maintenance may even be factors in some industries. *But the heart of application expertise lies with the people at the customer interface*—the sales force (as at Nordstrom or Home Depot or H-P) or the people in customer service (Airborne Express, Mack Trucks) or the people in technical support (Microsoft, Water Pik). These companies may well have products with certain strong features, but they stake their claims, their competitive advantages, on their abilities to ascertain customer needs and forge a custom linkage between those needs and the products or services available. *Whereas the focal point of excellence in product superiority is often R&D or some derivative thereof, the focal point of excellence in application is often the sales and / or service corps of the enterprise.* Think what a difference there is between the two mind sets required!

As with its partners in the Competitive Triangle, application expertise doesn't just happen. It is the product of conscious choice by thoughtful business builders. The alternative to being all things to all people is to be some things to some people. Like the pursuit of product superiority, application excellence is likely to be a hollow gesture if done faintheartedly or on a stop/start basis. Focus is required. Skill in understanding and responding to customer needs must be cultivated over time. It is virtually impossible to muster enough resources to excel simultaneously in both product features *and* application assistance. A trade-off has to be made. Is the company's competitive advantage to be built on being first into the marketplace with what is new? Or is it to be built on being second or so in line with perhaps fewer features but a more customizable package? Which value is top dog, and do the blueprints for the enterprise reflect whatever decision is made? (Or do the blueprints remain silent on the subject...or hedge?)

The fact of the matter is that most businesses need to have some minimum level of both product performance *and* application support. The most technically advanced software or medicine in the world will not sell well for long if there is no one to call or see for help in using it. And a sales force of application PhDs will not deliver a competitive advantage if its line of mousetraps is vastly inferior. *The trick is to excel on one point of the triangle and to be "good enough" on the other two.*

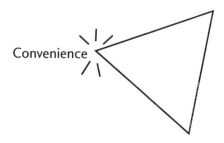

CONVENIENCE

What does this mean? Convenience takes many forms. Is it easy to do business with you? (It is with L.L. Bean, Wal Mart, Fidelity, or Boeing.) Is using your company's service or products relatively effortless when compared to what competitors offer? (Southwest Airlines, Teledyne Water Pik, Caterpillar.) Do customers feel comfortable and confident when dealing with your organization? (Charles Schwab; McDonald's; Saturn.) Does your offering provide a complete solution? For example, picture a mousetrap that comes complete with...

1) a special cheese that is precut in trap-size pieces;
2) a disposable bag for the deceased rodent; and
3) a CD ROM on the art of mice entrapment by Dr. Felix Katt, a famous catcher.

The mousetrap maker with such a total solution may be a winner in the marketplace—especially if no competitor makes dealing with mice so easy, so relatively simple, so convenient. In one way or another, convenience can distinguish a "me-too" product or service from competitive offerings in ways that produce tangible business results. Here are a couple of examples of convenience.

Question: What are the top three rules of successful retailing? Answer: Location, location, location! Why? Because location equates directly to customer convenience. If you have a store that is difficult to reach (or hard to park near), the best products or the most skilled sales people in the world are unlikely to make you a winner in the rough & tumble of retailing. Nordstrom with its legendary customer pampering would be just another department store if potential customers had to walk a mile to shop. (At its big-city sites, Nordstrom provides valet parking!)

Why are mail order companies continuing to take market share from retail stores? Convenience. What is one secret of the Internet's appeal? Convenience. This form of competitive advantage has many facets. Convenience can usefully be thought of as that combination of product selection, ease of doing business, and reliability which gives customers the **lowest total cost** (hard dollar + hassle) over the lifetime of their exposure. Authors Treacy and Wiersema put it this way:

> *Lowest total cost? It can mean lowest price, but it doesn't always. What it does mean is that when all the costs to the customer of owning and using the company's product or service are added up—costs such as price, time spent at the checkout counter, the inconvenience of untimely repair—nobody else's deal is likely to be any better.*[8]

Or, perhaps, as good.

A few years back, Sunset Designs was an emerging company that made and marketed home sewing kits across the U.S. The company was well known for the originality and freshness of its product designs. In fact, the company employed on either a direct or free-lance basis some of the most outstanding handwork artists in the country. Yet the senior builders of the business consciously decided to build Sunset's *primary* competitive advantage on the basis of a broad inventory and lightning-fast delivery service to retailers. This choice was made after a lot of head scratching and deliberation about the actual reasons both consumers and retailers buy and the possible ways to gain a lasting competitive advantage in an industry characterized by many small, cottage-type competitors. Their analysis indicated that both ultimate customers and retailers like to buy on impulse from a wide selection of kits. Yes, superior designs had their place, but any given hot new design usually didn't stay hot for very long. Sunset had a strong balance sheet and the discipline required to build a sophisticated inventory and order-processing system capable of shipping incoming orders within twenty-four hours. The leaders of Sunset felt the steep money requirements would be beyond the reach of most of their competitors. They opted to focus on making it extremely easy to do business with Sunset. They developed a company that could identify and move high-demand items onto retailers' shelves in a fraction of the time of industry norms. Everyone came out ahead—except for Sunset Design's competitors.

Sunset's approach is the model for what many retailers and manufacturers are doing today.

Convenience doesn't just happen. It often—but not always—requires a lot of people doing a lot of things right time after time—"operational excellence" in the words of Treacy and Wiersema.

So, product superiority, application expertise, and convenience—these are the competitive magnets that attract customers. What about **price**? The sticker price of a product or service is usually the most visible part of the total cost. *All other things being equal*, price often carries the day. All other things do tend toward equality in established, mature markets, so price competition is often the norm. Low price used to walk arm in arm with low quality. No more. Low quality hardly can find a home in any industry these days. Now "value pricing" is the thing. It means that a sticker price must be compatible with the level of product performance, the application, and the overall convenience of the total ownership experience. Once again, all other things being roughly equal (between competitive offerings), price often carries the day. It the tie-breaker in me-too situations.

Perhaps the best way to put price—and, usually, the underlying cost picture—into perspective is to think of price as a companion of one of the three forms of competitive advantage.

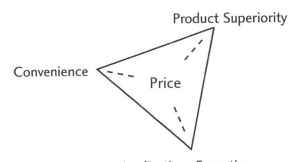

Competitive Triangle

If your emerging company is currently in me-too circumstances, your cost picture had best be healthy while you work to develop a *sustainable* competitive advantage.

At Dana Corporation, a mammoth manufacturer of medium-technology mechanical products, the theme for years has been productivity improvement. In one recent seven-year period, the company doubled its productivity. During the same period the output per hour worked by all the companies in the U.S. increased on average only 0.7% per year. Continually increasing productivity gave Dana a cost and price advantage while it worked on enhancing its engineering and development skills.

Why do start-up airline companies always initiate price wars? Because it is hard for airlines to differentiate themselves in any other way. But competing on price is most often a short-lived way to build a business. Consider this story from the *Wall Street Journal*.

At Airborne Express, going for growth was simply a matter of offering airfreight customers the lowest rates around. The carrier could afford to do so because its costs were the lowest in the industry. But as low prices helped Airborne Express gain market share, competitors such as Federal Express, the industry leader, struck back. The upshot: Several years of an on-again, off-again price war that lasted until mid-1995. "As they went after our customers, we went after theirs, first with aggressive pricing and then with more services and extended contracts, " said Jerry Cameron, Airborne's vice president of corporate accounts. By the time the war was over, the industry's prices were 20% below Airborne's original rate.

"No one wins a price war. You just try to hang on and survive," according to Cameron. "We ended up exchanging customers at lower yields."[2]

The bottom line is that price by itself is probably not a viable avenue along which to build an enterprise for the long haul deep into the 2000s.

Which one of the three forms of competitive advantage is most appropriate for an emerging company? There is no one-size-fits-all answer. Like a house or a barn or a boat or an athletic team, a competitive advantage is *built*. The best form for a given emerging company to build depends on the capabilities and tastes of the people therein as well as the operating environment. The message of this chapter has been merely that few companies with long term success patterns excel in more than one way *vis-a-vis* competition. Focus is required.

It's often difficult to get the hard-driving leaders of growth companies to give more than lip service to the fact that they need to pick and choose. But in Treacy & Wiersema's words, "Deep management concentration on one key business value..."[8] is one of the attributes that seems to go hand in hand with building a company for the long haul. To concentrate on building one form of competitive advantage at the expense of the others requires discipline and conviction. The conviction can often flow from—or at least be boosted by—sound strategic planning.

> **KEY POINT 5: Construct a sustainable competitive advantage over time.**

4
Pathways
to
Growth

"The difficulty in life is the choice."
- George Moore

The typical stages in the life cycle of an emerging company were covered in Chapter 1. Such companies are normally piloted in their earlier stages by ambitious souls who work long and hard to fill the cash and people voids exposed by either a sudden excess, or a continuing lack, of orders. In football parlance, the quarterbacks on the teams spend most of their time scrambling in pursuit of the next first down (purchase order) so they can keep a drive down the field toward the goal line going.

This chapter does not cover scrambling techniques. Rather it is aimed at providing a framework for systematically picking a path along which to pursue expectations. The material here is directed toward people building companies which have already graduated from the problems of month-to-month existence, i.e., meeting the next payroll. Such problems are intellectually simple compared to those that confront the senior people of an enterprise–a company or a division–that has edged into its industry's big leagues as a viable competitor. As *Business Week* put it in a cover article about emerging Sun Microsystems: "There is a downside to the triumph of Sun's network vision: Every computer maker now shares it (the vision) and is gunning for Sun." [9] Such an enterprise has a number of opportunities before it, limited resources, of course, and a host of new factors with which to contend. Some picking and choosing needs to be done. Focus is in order. The notion of a longer-range plan slips into the picture.

An early reaction to thinking beyond the current operating cycle is that the range of alternatives for building the business is infinite. Strategic planning has a mysterious sound to it implying that a certain wizardry is required. This impression is false. The basic pathways for building a business are finite and proven; they are six in number. Each revolves around the fundamental question of to whom will the emerging company sell what, the *sine qua non* of capitalism. They are depicted in the diagram, Six Basic Strategies for Building a Business.

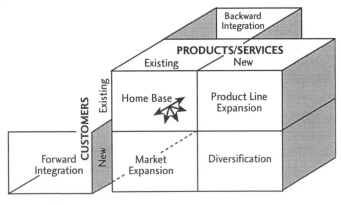

Six Basic Strategies for Building a Business

The six basic strategies include: Home Base, Product Line Expansion, Market Expansion, Forward Integration, Backward Integration, and Diversification. *In a competitive operating environment, each of the six requires a different recipe of specific skills and behavior if it is to be executed successfully over time.* People are the legs of strategy execution. People need to understand a strategy in order to execute it in harmony with one another. People can understand a lucid strategy better than a muddy one. This is one more reason focus is important in an emerging company where strategy execution can come unraveled in a blink.

KEY POINT 6 : Keep strategy simple.

Home Base

The starting point for building a business for tomorrow is what the enterprise is doing today: Home Base. Existing products and/or services are being sold to an existing set or type of customers. An upstate New York winery is selling its bottled output to consumers via supermarkets. A $100 million Phoenix consulting firm is selling contract research to various government agencies, the DOE, DOD, and DOT. A Palo Alto pharmaceutical company is selling ethical drugs to pharmacy wholesalers and promoting the products through physicians in certain selected medical specialties. When does it make sense to attempt to move off of Home Base, to alter a business strategy—or a corporate strategy if the entity is a one-business company? The answer is that a business-building team should generate plans to extend its strategy beyond the Home Base quadrant when a systematic analysis indicates that the enterprise can no longer meet its expectations by operating within that quadrant! It is a relatively straightforward proposition.

If you, the business builder, can get where you want to go by doing basically what you are already doing, don't venture onto new paths. On the other hand, if staying on Home Base means you are unlikely to fulfill your ambitions, then a choice must be made to break new ground–product line expansion, backward integration, or whatever.

Home Base is not a static quadrant. It may contain huge opportunities including closely related, untapped segments (with known competitors) and numerous niches (free of competitors). Staying at Home Base serving existing types of customers with existing products or services is most often the absolutely right choice, a key element of focusing your business. A Home Base strategy normally has plenty of room for all manner of product line extensions, market initiatives to acquire more of the same kinds of customers, and so on. It is the business you know best. Move away from it at your peril. If your company has a product that cures cancer in humans, you probably do not need to venture into new products for other diseases (e.g. heart disease) or into new markets (e.g. veterinary cancer) to successfully pursue your expectations!

The signal that a major change in strategy may be called for is illustrated in the diagram, Trajectory vs Expectations.

Trajectory vs. Expectations

Point A represents the starting point, the position of the emerging company at the time focusing and planning become agenda items. Point B represents the level of expectations at the edge of the planning horizon. When the projected Home Base Trajectory from Point A misses Point B in a significant way, a change in strategy may be worth considering. This diagram is a conceptual tool. The lines, particularly the Home Base Trajectory, are difficult to plot given all the variables in the operating environment. But what is the alternative to going through the mental gymnastics necessary to estimate the shape and location of these lines? The alternative is to wait and see what happens. Then to react...the antithesis of planning. Of course an emerging company wants to remain nimble and, to some extent, opportunistic, but increasing size and complexity require more brain work and less reliance on the legs!

The Level of Expectations is also a candidate for scrutiny, particularly in private companies. Here is an admonition from material developed by your author for entrepreneurs with early-stage companies:

Expand methodically from a profitable base toward a balanced business. *Optimism is both the poison and the antidote of the growth company manager. It may be possible to accomplish all things, but not simultaneously. With limited resources, sequential growth over time is the judicious prescription for prosperity. Seek logical, incremental extensions of existing activities, but avoid a growth-for-growth's-sake psychology. Bigger is not automatically better; more is not necessarily merrier. Make managing a competitive advantage. Increase customer dependency on the enterprise. Economic success can breed more of the same and/or other returns for the primary participants. Money is the traditional reward; life style considerations are becoming more widespread.*[10]

Consider the requirements of a sound decision to change strategy by moving off Home Base. (Once again, Home Base includes product-line extensions and market expansion at the margin, i.e. in small increments closely related to existing customers.) First, the business builders must know to whom they are selling what, now. Second, they need to have projections in which they have confidence about what is likely to happen to their business over the next few years. And third, they must have a reasonably clear picture of expectations–what the enterprise is to accomplish. Here is an example.

The leaders of a very successful specialty chemical company in the southeastern U.S.A. came to the conclusion that to continue their exciting sales growth, overseas expansion and major new equity money would be required. After a lot of analysis and soul-searching, they concluded that such moves would drastically alter their life styles as scientist-managers. These conclusions led to a decision to alter some of their financial objectives in favor of other objectives related to their professional and personal preferences. The board of the company agreed with the alterations. No change in basic strategy was initiated.

Suppose a conclusion is reached that a change in strategy *is* warranted in your company. Product line expansion and market expansion are the most popular basic strategies for growing a business beyond Home Base.

Product Line Expansion
Many start-ups during the last ten to twenty years have been based on black boxes or other single-product concepts. The new idea–a fail-safe computer, birth control pill, index mutual fund, resoleable athletic shoe, or an Internet search engine–provides the blast off. But it

seldom has sufficient power to provide sustained flight. Follow-on products (above and beyond line extensions) to extend the initial customer franchise become an option for the leadership of the business to consider. Many builders pick up the option. They pursue growth opportunities in the product line expansion quadrant. They seek to develop *or acquire* products new to the enterprise, products that can be sold to existing customers. Ski manufacturers tiptoe into outdoor clothing; outdoor clothing makers introduce lines of jewelry; jewelry companies add fashionable sun glasses to their offerings; and sun glasses manufacturers try sporting goods.

When vigorously pursued as the primary strategy for building the business, product line expansion requires people with certain talents which are otherwise not needed. For example, blue-sky research people may not be required in companies sticking to the Home Base quadrant. But a company intent on growth via the internal development of distinctly new products may well need such researchers. If a decision is made to expand the product line via external sources, e.g. through acquisition or joint ventures, people with proven talent in these activities are needed.

Once an expanded product line starts to take shape, related operating issues such as product introductions, servicing, pricing, and inventory policies arise. They can lead to organization design questions as well as outright conflicts as the enterprise is pulled away from its home base and proven competencies. A lead article in the *Wall Street Journal* tells it like it is:

> *A major challenge facing many managements is to balance the need for significant new-product innovation with the need to keep expansion from running amok. Despite promising market research, most new products fail.*[2]

The point is that choosing to grow via product line expansion, if done conscientiously, means the fundamental nature of the company must be reshaped appropriately. Here is an additional comment from the *WSJ* article:

> *Half of those (new product) launches don't reach sales goals because of how they are sold. "A common pitfall," says Jerome Colletti of the Alexander Group, "is to assume a new product can be sold effectively by the current sales force. Just as much time should be spent in choosing the right sales team, compensation program, and sales approach as in choosing customer prospects."*[2]

A shift in strategy from home base to product line expansion is a nontrivial event. If commitment to the new strategy is fainthearted, chances are good that half-measures will prevail. Plans will not be executed well. Previous success will be tainted. This is not a formula for long-term business happiness in an emerging company up against determined, capable competitors.

Market Expansion

New territory—one form of market expansion—is as old as business itself: start locally; expand regionally; go national; become global. Most of the exploration of the physical world between the fifteenth and nineteenth centuries was sponsored (and financed) by business people seeking new geographic markets for their goods. Today, from fast-food companies and banks to accounting firms, software companies, and category-killer retailers, market expansion is the strategy of choice. For example, the Bahlsen company of Hanover, Germany opened a pilot group of retail cookie and bakery specialty shops in U.S.A. malls to capitalize on the cookie boom. And one of the largest insurance companies in America recently completed and committed itself to a strategic plan based almost completely on opportunities around the Pacific.

New territory is just one of several possibilities in the market expansion quadrant–existing products for distinctly new customers. Another possibility is expansion into totally new segments. A company selling computers to businesses might enter the consumer market segment. Another possibility is expansion into new channels of distribution. For example, a company selling clothing via its own retail stores might inaugurate a mail order operation. Another possibility would be expansion via reaching out to different price points. Today both Mercedes-Benz and BMW are introducing lower-priced versions of their luxury cars in attempts to grow their revenues with sales to car buyers of more modest tastes or means than traditional Mercedes-Benz or BMW customers.

A strategy of market expansion, like any of the six basic strategies, requires certain capabilities that are not necessarily in the inventory of the emerging company. For example, geographic expansion may exasperate decision making. Selling into new channels may require delivery/pricing/inventory systems and services that are radically different to the people of the company. More than one high-tech company has been burned when it attempted to sell versions of its industrial products to consumers via retailers.

The problems with a major change in strategy are solvable, but resources are required. This fact of life highlights the need to make strategy selection a serious matter. It's most often pure folly to go timidly into a major market or product line expansion effort. It is even worse to go halfheartedly in several directions at once! On the top of the next page is a diagram, Two-Path

Growth Strategy. Draw a heavy diagonal line through it to help yourself remember to avoid such an approach to building your business.

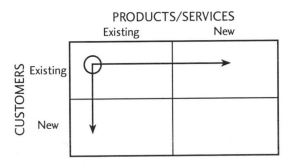

Two-Path Growth Strategy

It is possible for an emerging company to grow with a two-path strategy. But it is a risky way to build. With such an approach, the construction job becomes quite complicated. Often increased complexity leads to organizational constipation. Deadlines and budgets are missed. In simpler times the deadlines would have been met by dint of extra effort on the part of the key people. But an emerging company may already be too large for fire-drill fixes except in the case of an occasional grand-slam emergency. One of the senior planning tasks in an emerging company is to review strategy and settle on a new pathway when there is a good reason to do so. This is central to getting and keeping focus in the business. It is easy to drift around in and off of home base in the rush of events that accompany building a business. Fuzzy strategy is difficult to execute. The same is true for start/stop strategy. Budgets may change year to year; strategy should be relatively stable. Focus is required.

There are three other basic strategies for building a business. Two of them are forms of "vertical" integration.

Forward Integration & Backward Integration

Forward integration occurs when a company stretches from home base toward its ultimate customers. For example, today there is a proliferation of Factory Outlet stores in which brand-name manufacturers open and operate their own retail stores.

Backward integration occurs when a company either acquires one or more of its suppliers or invests in facilities to replace those suppliers with its own operation. Backward integration from home base can be undertaken as a means of growing or of guaranteeing needed resources, or both.

Vertical integration in one direction or the other has been around as a growth strategy since the early days of industrialization when the original set of emerging companies (steel, autos, chemicals, oil) were pieced together as "fully integrated" enterprises. In general, the trend today is away from integration and toward more and more disintegration, "outsourcing" as it is called. In part, this is a product of focusing, i.e. of trying to concentrate on doing a limited number of things very well.

Diversification

This last basic strategy is the most difficult to pull off successfully because it generally requires business builders to operate far from their proven platforms of competence. Growth through diversification—new products *and* new markets simultaneously—is taxing, to put it mildly. The Honor Roll of Bad Strategy is full of ill-fated diversification offenses by (previously) effective business builders. The Honor Roll includes the management team that entered the field of cosmetics as an adjunct to the team's successful food business. There are the metal can entrepreneurs who thought they could do well making hit records, and the diesel motors executives who bought a ski manufacturer. And not to be forgotten are a slew of movie moguls who thought the broadcast TV business would be a walk in the park. Diversification is a tough strategy to execute well over time. It is about as far as you can get from finding a protected niche you know and filling it. But sometimes diversification is necessary.

For example, changes in government regulations can put the future of an industry in jeopardy. Affected builders alert to the changing times might wisely choose to broaden the bases of their enterprises via a strategy of diversification. The nuclear reactor industry is a case in point. General Atomic Co. was for years a leader in one advanced technology for nuclear power plants. But the market for all forms of public utility nuclear power was gradually regulated out of existence. General Atomic leadership had little choice from a rational business standpoint but to redirect its impressive human resources (1,000 engineers and scientists) into new areas of endeavor. Over time, G.A. shifted into contract research, consulting, and the development of nonnuclear energy products. In the years ahead, regulation could strangle (and create) other industries.

Advances in technology can also clear-cut what was once a forest of opportunity. Computers on a chip replaced mechanical adding machines, once the backbone of a huge industry. Preemptive diversification might have been an informed choice by the senior people in the affected companies. Diversification has its place, but in general, among the six basic pathways, it is the strategy of last resort for a typical emerging company.

The Search for the Right Strategy

As a class of people, emerging company people are a smart, hardworking, achievement-oriented bunch. But the class in its entirety includes only the standard allocation of wizards and geniuses. With a rare exception, everyone in the class puts his or her pants on one leg at a time. So what? The "so what" is that too much stress can be put on choosing just the "right strategy." There is usually more than one way to build a company successfully. The trick is to pick a strategy and then stick to it and make it work. In others words, focus your business. In large measure, it is the effective execution of a chosen strategy that puts the winners out in front of the losers in a competitive situation. In professional football, to paraphrase Vince Lombardi, the team that runs, blocks, passes, and tackles well, consistently, is going to come out on top. In an emerging company, the construction team that outlines a clear picture of expectations, systematically chooses a discrete form of competing and a pathway for growth, and then commits its resources to go down that pathway, has good odds of achieving the expectations.

KEY POINT 7: **Support decisions with commitments.**

5

Summary
Chapters 1-4

"We've got to disturb the present."
- Roberto Goizueta,
CEO, Coca Cola Co.[11]

The challenge to builders of an emerging company is to continually adjust everything to fit the oncoming flow of new realities. Often the flow becomes a flood for two reasons. First, corporations, in general, are the focal point of rapid social and technological change. Second, growth itself accelerates the rate of change. It is quite safe to assume that much of what worked well yesterday will not work as well tomorrow. As Bill Walsh who is credited with building the modern San Francisco 49ers professional football organization puts it:

Life isn't fair. To repeat success, you can hardly ever do exactly what worked so well before.[12]

Planning is an attempt to determine a course of action through or around the flood. It is an antidote to confusion and MBH, managing by hope. *Strategic* planning deals with issues in the rare air above the normal operating cycle. It has to do with continually repositioning a business at the moving intersection of opportunity and capability. Sound planning leads to thoughtful decisions about where to invest and divest cash and key people.

It is often hard for a busy person to step back away from the day-to-day fray in order to spend time on abstract, strategic planning matters. Perspective is required: The ante in sales dollars to enter the Fortune 500 class of companies is much larger than it used to be. Most successful enterprises pass through a variety of crises and stages of growth enroute to maturity. Explicit objectives are the threshold for strategy formulation. Clear expectations are a necessity, not an elective, in an enterprise of any complexity. Excelling in some (one) way to build a sustainable competitive advantage requires discipline. And finally, the number of basic pathways for building a business is finite; there are six to be precise. Once a point of excellence and a pathway are chosen, the body and mind of the emerging company need to be shaped to execute what is now the strategy for building the business. Payoff depends on execution.

At the corporate level of a multibusiness company, much of a strategic planning effort is directed first at establishing boundaries: What business or businesses shall we be in...and not in. Then, second, those involved must pick and choose where to invest and divest among the various possibilities.

At the business level, or at the corporate level of a single-business company, the process is much the same: Boundaries first, picking and choosing second. Only now the units under discussion—the planning units—are different. More on this in the next chapter. At either level, corporate or business, the seven key points suggested in the preceding chapters apply. They are restated below in an action format to facilitate their use.

KEY POINTS
1. Identify and use a common vocabulary within your company.
2. Consciously separate the different levels of planning: corporate, business, and functional.
3. Increase the proportion of energy devoted to planning as your enterprise grows in size and complexity.
4. Structure expectations throughout your organization.
5. Construct a sustainable competitive advantage over time.
6. Keep strategy simple.
7. Support decisions with commitments.

Preview
Chapters 6-10

It is easy for successful companies to become unfocused. Most builders of businesses are opportunistic, and opportunities pop up all over the place. Planning is the discipline you use to maintain or regain focus as your emerging enterprise increases in size and complexity. The chapters that follow provide a methodology for working through the muddle in search of the best way to be *only* some things to some people.

The mechanics of strategic planning are not rocket science. First, you need to disaggregate your busy and, perhaps, complicated business into planning units–workable, discrete parts for analysis. Then you need to develop a comprehensive, thoughtful point of view about each unit using one or more planning techniques. Finally, the whole collection of information needs to be served up, consumed, and digested enroute to decisions about where best to invest and divest the cash and people of the business for years ahead.

A solid planning process is the best groundwork for effective plan execution.

6
Selecting Planning Units

"Divide and rule."
- Machiavelli

Strategic planning is a discipline of systematically sorting through a company and deciding what roles its component parts are to play in the future of the enterprise. To focus is to choose. Normally there will be both keepers and discards. To collect and analyze data enroute to decisions on a plan of action, the responsible planning team needs to divide the business into pieces or units that can be compared. Most often in a mature company the units for comparison will be the operating profit centers. This means the planning units will be the existing organizational units. In an emerging company, however, there may be but one operating profit center (the whole company), or any profit centers that do exist—regions or product lines, for example—may be happenstance and less than ideal for thinking strategically about the future.

Consider this example. One of Silicon Valley's finest young semiconductor companies was at $70 million in sales and growing at a rate of about 30% per year, compounded. This emerging company had the following characteristics:

- Six major product lines sold throughout the world.
- Three geographic profit centers: U.S., Europe, Far East. Each had a general manager who reported to the president.
- Three functional vice-presidents (marketing, R&D, finance) who reported to the president.
- Two major process technologies in which the company excelled.
- Four major groupings (segments) of customers: Government, aerospace, industrial companies, consumer companies.

Assuming a desire to do so, how should the leaders update and upgrade their plan for the business? It's a tough but vital question, and the people in this example followed a fairly standard progression of learning over a four-year period. "Looking back," one participant said, "it was a little like trying get your arms around an elephant!"

The planning team's **first pass** at developing a strategic plan revolved around three-year plans drafted by each of the functional vice-presidents. The drafts were interesting. They were combined into large, three-ring binders full of material which the planning team of seven reviewed and discussed in great detail. The result was a slightly more farsighted budget for the coming year and a set of performance numbers for the subsequent two years. However, once the annual budget was finalized, the three-ring binders were not opened again. Management continued to build the company on all fronts: three profit centers around the world, six product lines, two technologies, four segments.

The next year, a new round of strategic planning had a somewhat greater sense of urgency. It was becoming obvious to a growing number of people in positions of leadership that some of the company's internal systems were being stretched to the breaking point. Critical monthly performance information was slow in coming; inventory turns were drooping; and quarterly R&D dollar-allocation meetings were turning into regular shouting matches. This **second pass** at a more strategic plan relied heavily on input from the three profit-center general managers. It was their turn to peer into the dim future and prepare three-ring binders full of information and thoughts.

Once again, the review of material and discussions among the participants was useful. The consensus was that the main product on this pass should be an improved annual plan for the coming year and some shrinking of the territory over which the R&D people could roam—a smidgen of focus, to be sure! More money was allocated to upgrading the internal operating systems with an eye to the $130 million sales figure now projected for the third year out.

From this brief description, can you, honored reader, estimate the extent to which the questions in the Planning Diamond (page 15) were being asked and answered by the planning team?

Here they are:

1. What are the internal and external realities?
2. What are we trying to accomplish?
3. How shall we pursue our expectations for the business?
4. How shall we orchestrate our resources to actually execute our plan?

The raw material for the first pass at a more strategic plan came from the functional chiefs; for the second pass it came from the profit-center chiefs. Therefore, in succession, by default, the primary planning units were first the functional units of the business and later the profit centers. Focusing a business requires making choices, and as a practical matter, serious keep/discard choices have got to be between parts of the enterprise that are potentially discardable. The planning team in this example worked itself into a bit of a box. It was not in the cards to stop doing one or more of the functions, e.g., to drop R&D in favor of marketing. Neither was it possible (at the time) to disengage one of the three profit centers, e.g., get out of Europe to concentrate on the USA and the Far East. (Please note, however, that dropping either internal R&D or Europe would have been a major step to focus the business, the subject of this book. But such extreme surgery was outside the thinking of the people at the time.)

Serious trade-off discussions and decisions between potentially discardable parts of the business could not be made because those parts were not on the table. They were not in the view finder! This does not mean that the planning work that was done was useless. It had important value in that it led to decisions about product lines, pricing, refinements in the marketing strategy, R&D priorities, and, to some extent, the placement of key people. It was planning, but it was not strategic planning. It resulted in numerous changes and adjustments "at the margin." But in this case two passes at planning did not generate illuminating, hard choices related directly to capabilities, opportunities, and the competitive position of the company a few years ahead.

What are a few examples of such hard choices? The company excelled in two process technologies. Could it keep up the pace in both, or should it drop one? The same question applied to the three product technologies nurtured by R&D: Could the company keep pace? The $100 million enterprise was selling into four big segments, an average of $25 million per segment. Could it gain and maintain an adequate market share (very important in the semiconductor business) in all four? Or was debilitating dilution a prospect? The ambitious builders were reaching around the globe at the same time the domestic competitive environment was boiling. Could the company do battle successfully on multiple battle fronts?

These are examples of **strategic issues**. A planning process keyed to operating people and fueled primarily with operating data of their choosing will end up dealing with operating matters, which are essentially tactical. They are important, but tactical matters are best dealt with in the context of a strategic plan. Otherwise there is a 50/50 chance people will end up pulling hard in conflicting directions as they go about their work.

Here is a final word in this story of an emerging company. In real life, the expectations for the business were very simple: *More*. More sales, more margin, more profits, more people, more products, more territory. You name it. And all the participants plotted their courses from this guiding star. The unspoken assumption was that within its historical framework, this emerging semiconductor company would sell (almost) everything to everybody. The story has a relatively happy ending, however.

The planning units of the first two passes were not viable for *strategic* planning. During the third year, after seeing the second year's set of binders gather dust from January on, the top team settled on six major product categories as the planning units. The categories cut across organizational lines in all directions, i.e. across profit centers, functional departments, and technologies. The product categories were not organizational units. This made for some administrative difficulties during the planning process, but for this company the six product categories provided the basis for a real three-year strategic plan from which the various business (organizational) chiefs then prepared annual plans. The builders actually dropped one product category and staged a quiet withdrawal from another, moves which greatly simplified the business and released resources to apply to the chosen areas of emphasis.

As a matter of interest, the enterprise was acquired some years later by a large European corporation, in part, because the buyers were impressed with the "disciplined approach" of the management team to growth.

What are the criteria for selecting planning units? They are four in number. Each discrete planning unit should...

1. Lend itself readily to the collection of data about market opportunities, specific competitors, investment requirements, risks, government regulation, technology trends, and other factors related to the requirements for performance (sales, profits, ROI, etc.) in the future. A more complete list of possible data points will be presented in the next three chapters.

2. Be reasonably comparable to other planning units in terms of keep/discard decisions. Cars and trucks might be OK as planning units; cars and oil well services would be difficult to work with in an operating company. (Investment firms such as holding companies, insurance companies, and conglomerates are a special case beyond the scope of this book.)

3. *Facilitate implementation* once decisions are reached about the role of the unit in the company's future. Generally speaking, a planning unit should have a boss. That is, overall responsibility for executing a unit's plan should be assignable to an individual, or in rare instances, a team.

4. *Be intrinsic to the life of the business*. Planning units should be *the* fundamental building blocks. This means they should capture how the planners really think about the business when all the managerial apparatus is stripped away. Perhaps the heart of an upstart airline is its route structure; a young consulting firm, its practices; a medical device venture, its professional disciplines.

Here is another relevant case history.

The ambitious senior people in a research-driven, Eastern pharmaceutical company ($500 million sales worldwide) tried over several years to get a strategic planning program going. They used their seven regions (profit centers) around the world as the planning units. The regional structure and staffing was mandatory because each country in which the company operated had vastly different regulatory procedures and sensitivities. Annually, with a lot of computer-graphics fanfare and expensive travel, a strategic planning dance was held. The regional vice-presidents presented their thoughts on the future. A lot of discussion ensued. Then, later in the agenda, everyone present was told by the senior research people (from the central lab) precisely which products would be researched, produced, and introduced in the various regions during the planning period. After a few years of this the company stalled.

Because of the stall, the leaders made a change; they declared that, henceforth, therapy areas (heart disease, dermatology, etc.) would be the primary planning units.

(case continued on next page)

> This move led, for the first time, to meaningful discussions between the central researchers and the regional organizations. The discussions opened the way to some truly strategic decisions. The real breakthrough came when a decision was made to actually get out of two (of nine) therapy areas in order to better focus the business.

Like most higher-growth companies, this pharmaceutical company had a need to clean house periodically, to prune back the range of its products, markets, and projects so that a critical mass of proven capability could be marshaled and channeled into the selected few opportunities most compatible with achieving the expectations for the company. Such prunings, however, are not painless. There are seldom historical activities within an organization that do not have strong advocates. A handy litmus test for the seriousness of a strategic planning effort is quite simply: **Was any truly significant pruning done?** Walking away from traditional parts of a business takes a lot of discipline.

There is one other lesson from the pharmaceutical company story. After the stall, a senior officer was assigned worldwide, planning responsibility for each therapy area. He or she had to develop a picture of the global operating environment for, say, heart disease...no small task! This meant the planning units became a temporary overlay on the organization chart. But they were for "planning reasons only." The overlays led to some turf battles in the early part of the initiative, but the end result—a hard, global look at the therapy areas intrinsic to the enterprise—satisfied everyone. A year or so later the global therapy leaders became a permanent part of the structure of the company.

Once again, as a matter of interest, the company did achieve its ambitious expectations for the planning period, including a billion in sales.

Organizational units (profit centers, functional departments) are typically the first choice as planning units; they may well satisfy numbers one, two, and three on the list of criteria. But number four, intrinsicness, is *highly* desirable, if not essential. One way or another, a planning team needs to get at the basic, organic building blocks of its business. When it does, it usually becomes apparent that different products, services, divisions, markets, technologies, or combinations of these have different longer-term potentials for the enterprise. Putting selected pieces together in a synergistic, coherent way is high art for the professional business person. Discrete planning units are the ingredients of alternative strategic scenarios. Your choice of planning units directly affects the possibilities that emerge in a sound planning process.

7
Hierarchy of Planning Techniques
Part I of III

*"What Bethune has brought to Continental
Airlines is a single-minded focus..."*
- Business Week

Given all the publicity on planning it is easy to get the impression that it is something new. Yet a look at the history of entrepreneurship and enterprise in general shows that thinking ahead—in terms of what shall be sold and to whom—is as old as business itself. True builders of businesses have always done it. They had to. Every great company you can think of started small selling something to somebody. To be sure, the tools and techniques of analysis have become more sophisticated. But that doesn't automatically make the newer approaches better for a given company. In the same way that a professional golfer has to select the right club for a given shot, the professional business person responsible for sorting through and thinking about a total enterprise has to select appropriate techniques to analyze and determine the relative importance of his or her planning units.

In the pages that follow, a hierarchy of planning techniques will be presented. The higher up a technique is in the hierarchy, the more recent and more complicated it is to use.

An important question to consider when starting toward the strategic planning woods is this: On what basis will trade-off decisions be made enroute to a comprehensive strategy for pursuing expectations?

Intuition

By far the oldest and most common way of making decisions about a longer-term direction is to rely on the buried experience and judgment of the most knowledgeable people in the enterprise. Referring to the pair of touchdowns that gave the Pittsburgh Steeler's a dramatic victory in Super Bowl XIV, pro football quarterback Terry Bradshaw said:

Both times that down-the-center pass play just seemed like a good thing to try. It was a new play for us; but it worked.

Intuition at work.

Many major opportunities anchored in the tomorrows are not—and will not be—obvious or discoverable; no amount of market research will ferret them out. Leaps of faith are required. It is unlikely that any key decision to pursue one opportunity over another will ever be completely quantitative. Sixth senses come into play. They bypass or transcend rational thinking, skip over it. Your intuitive people may be neither ambitious nor gregarious. Their thoughts need to be coaxed into the open. People often don't know ideas even exist until they are verbalized. They pop out under the right conditions. In your strategic planning, therefore, make room for some free-form thinking; smother or deride intuition at your peril. It can be a source of valuable insights as your business moves into the 21st century.

Sales Volume

Push what's selling. Second in age and probably as common in practice as intuition are decisions based on the projected sales volumes of the planning units—whether they are product lines, divisions, markets or some combination. Longer-term bets in terms of what kinds of plants to build, which markets to enter, and where to invest research dollars are commonly a reflection of what is expected to be best for sales growth. If salient facts about all the budding companies in the world were put into a single data base along with the right algorithm, chances are good that the printout would look like this:

Relative Percentage of Resources Allocated to Planning Unit

Relative Sales Volume of Planning Unit

The virtue of using sales volume as the primary sorting technique is its simplicity. Its drawback, however, is that population and economic trends are fickle, technology is causing all sorts of unpredictable waves around the world, and the value systems at all buying points in the business food chain seem to be in continuous flux.

This combination makes projecting sales increasingly difficult and weakens sales volume as a strategic planning technique despite its popularity. Here's the way George Gilder, a senior fellow at the Discovery Institute in Seattle, describes the new millennium:

> *PCs linked by global networks like the Internet represent a tremendous, double force at the core of the world economy that will blow away all the established hierarchies and replace them with a new economy based on individual productivity.*[13]

Profitability

At the third step in the hierarchy interest shifts to profitability, the bottom line of an operating statement. Today a great many going concerns operate on the basis of an annual *profit* plan. This is a natural progression. Increasing sales revenue can cover a lot of problems for a period of time, but sooner or later most businesses need to make a solid, predictable profit. As a planning team looks out beyond the current budget cycle, it is logical that the projected profitability of the various units be factored into the analysis.

In 1987, the management team of an up & coming Midwestern company that made mining, pollution control, and fluid-handling equipment undertook a strategic planning effort separate from its traditional, annual, profit-planning cycle. The purpose was to explore a course for the nineties that would make full use of the momentum built up over the previous seven years. During that time the company had grown from $70 million to $425 million in sales. For the planning effort, the entire company was thoughtfully broken into twenty-seven planning units. Then, for the first time, the management team looked in detail beneath the three group aggregations of mining, pollution control, and fluid handling. The senior people were surprised to find that over a third of the twenty-seven units were actually unprofitable, and almost another third were only marginally profitable. It was also news to them to find that of the seven units with the best profit projections over the planning period, five were the responsibility of the most conservative and least aggressive of the company's three group leaders.

This short example reveals one desired attribute of a proper planning process that adds spice to it, namely, uncovering strategic lightning bolts. They illuminate! Suddenly there is insight and understanding about the hard realities of the business that years of grinding through an annual budgeting process would never reveal.

Cliff Morton, once the Vice-President of planning at Boise Cascade, recounts one lightning bolt in his experience. For years the construction team of an important consumer-products division (a planning unit) projected the division's sales and profits primarily on the basis of the population growth in the geographic area the division served. One year, however, a scheduled closer look at the bedrock details of what made the business tick turned up the fact that population growth had virtually nothing to do with the performance of the division. The real stimulus was the disposable income in the area which was tied to farm prices—a very different leading indicator for the business than population growth.

Contribution Margin

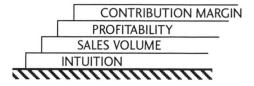

Contribution margin is a somewhat more sophisticated sorting technique than sales or profitability in that it involves a look at dollars "contributed" to the sum of the fixed cost plus the absolute profits of the enterprise.

Contribution Margin = Net Sales Price - Variable Costs

This technique has a lot of applicability in younger companies which have yet to install full cost accounting systems and/or which have simple product groups as the planning units. For example, a contribution margin analysis can reveal ways of increasing profits at a specified volume of sales by simply altering the product mix sold to produce that level of sales. In general, the effective use of contribution margin as a method of analysis draws attention to issues such as variable costs, fixed cost, pricing, product mix, and break-even points. These can be vital, strategic issues. Break-even considerations can be particularly important in an emerging company that is expanding willy-nilly with full confidence that tomorrow will look a lot like yesterday...or even better. *Nimbleness is inversely proportional to the height of the break-even point of the business.*

The three techniques above intuition in the hierarchy are essentially single-factor measures. They emigrate from the accounting function where data on sales, profitability, and margins is massaged. The next step in the hierarchy is a big one in that it is composed of two factors, profit *and* the dollars required (invested) to produce it.

Return on Investment (ROI)

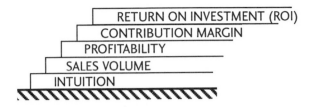

RETURN ON INVESTMENT (ROI)
CONTRIBUTION MARGIN
PROFITABILITY
SALES VOLUME
INTUITION

ROI analyses of planning units has caught hold with many builders of growth companies. Such people, along with stockholders and Wall Street veterans, have become increasingly interested not only in *How well is the business doing?* but also in *How much investment is it taking to do the job?* ROI analysis has been in vogue for many years as input to capital investment decisions; today it is being used to examine both current performance and strategic issues. ROI is a powerful, performance measuring stick. For example, which planning unit, X or Y, is the more attractive based on the information shown in the table below?

	X	**Y**
Sales Last Yr	$20,000,000	$30,000,000
Sales Growth over Previous Yr.	50%	20%
Profit % on Sales	15%	10%
Market Position	Strong	Strong
Outlook for Business	Excellent	Excellent

If you had limited resources to invest and had to choose one unit over the other to build (invest in) for the long haul, would you select X or Y?

Would your answer be the same if you knew that at present the investment dollars required to support unit X is $10,000,000; the amount required for unit Y is as much?

Said another way, it takes one dollar of investment to generate a two dollars of sales and 30 cents in profits in unit X; but a dollar of investment in unit Y produces six dollars of sales and 60 cents in profit. This means you get twice the bang for the buck, so to speak, in Y. The point is that ROI incorporates an additional factor, the amount of investment required, into the sorting process that is central to strategic planning. Sales, profits, and margins alone do not directly reflect the fact that it takes money to make money.

In summary to this point, the four steps immediately above intuition in the hierarchy tend to be based on internally generated data. Such data are relatively easy to come by and to assimilate compared to the three steps that follow in the next chapter.

8

Hierarchy of Planning Techniques

Part II

"Laura Ashley's Ann Iverson has restored profits and refocused on the home."

- Business Week

Product Life Cycle (PLC)

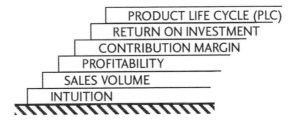

PRODUCT LIFE CYCLE (PLC)
RETURN ON INVESTMENT
CONTRIBUTION MARGIN
PROFITABILITY
SALES VOLUME
INTUITION

The PLC is the first sorting technique in the hierarchy to require a close look at what is going on outside the company in the marketplace. Extensive research over the years has shown that most products follow an S-shaped curve (see diagram on next page) over their life spans. Time, the horizontal axis, varies for different products. For example, the total life cycle time for Pet Rocks or Pong games was very short; the life cycle for the Ford 150 pickup trucks introduced in 1980 ran for 15 years. The shape of the normal PLC curve and its major stages are shown below.

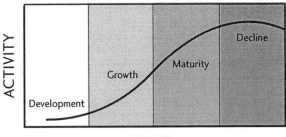

Again, time–months, years, decades–is the horizontal axis. Activity–the vertical axis–means the number of projects, competitors, sales transactions, or other measures of interest in the marketplace. Activity is an indicator of the visibility of the product or service.

A new idea starts out one way or another and goes through a period of **Development**. It may be a very short period (hula hoops) or an extended period (birth control pills). Whatever the length, many new ideas that withstand the tests of development are launched, and to the extent they are accepted in the marketplace, they enter a period of **Growth**–the second phase of the PLC. This phase may be long and gradual (golf clubs) or short and steep (CB radios). In either case, a point of inflection is eventually reached and the rate of growth decelerates; the product is edging into **Maturity**. By this time, competitive activity is often high and margins may be squeezed. Some competitors depart from the fray by choice (they decide to focus on other opportunities!), and other competitors are forced out due to their expensive cost structures.

There are sages who claim there are no mature markets, only mature managers with bent opportunity antennas. For example, pianos, watches, and motor cycles were all labeled mature once. All are enjoying growth again today. Actually, extending the growth phase and avoiding maturity *is* high art that typically requires new users, new uses, or repositioning the product via solid enhancements and/or advertising. The renaissance in motor cycles started when Honda reached out to a whole new segment of potential cycle buyers with: "You meet the nicest people on a Honda." Today you have to order it and wait for months to buy a new cycle.

Business builders arraying their planning units on a PLC curve for the first time will often find the ensuing discussion an event to remember. Suppose your enterprise has ten planning units and your analysis indicates the ten fall out in *one* of the three ways shown below.

What if your business is in this situation...

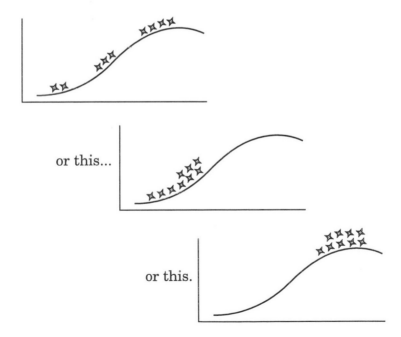

or this...

or this.

In each case the strategic implications are quite different. The top PLC diagram shows a set of planning units well into their life cycles. The resource allocation in a business with this situation should probably be quite unlike that in the second situation or the third.

With regard to planning techniques, here is an important point. Chances are that any PLC analysis of planning units will give you a significantly different picture of your business than, for example, a ROI analysis. Why? Because, by nature, older established planning units tend to have higher and, therefore, more favorable ROI's than younger ones. One reason is that the depreciation costs are lower for the older units. But the older units will also fall nearer the maturity phase of the PLC curve. So, there is a conflict: Higher ROI & Maturity vs. Lower ROI & Growth. Which technique, ROI or PLC, should be given preference by a strategic planning team? The answer is that probably neither should be used exclusively. Each can be helpful in thinking about, and then planning, the further construction of the business.

It is also possible to play with combinations of techniques in the hierarchy. Suppose ROI and PLC were combined and the planning units of, say, a book publishing company were plotted as shown in the diagram at the top of the next page. The size of the circles is proportional to the sales volumes of the units.

What are the implications of this two-factor analysis to a perceptive planning team? Are the highest ROI units (Multimedia, Reference Books) most deserving of significant additional investment? Should the Children's Books unit be injected with capital or the publisher's sharpest managers in order to turn it around (increase ROI) and restart it for growth? Does the 16% ROI for Trade Books give it a cloudy future even though it is early in the growth phase of the PLC? Interesting issues.

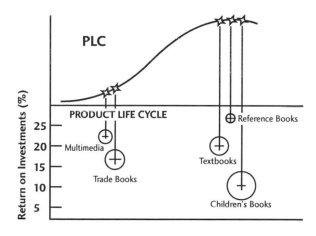

PLC and ROI

A thorough airing is the only road to informed decisions. Such issues–flushed out in the open with techniques–provide the grist for the strategic planning mill.

Experience Curve/Market Share

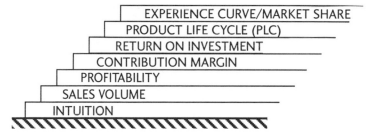

In recent times, no other single planning concept has received more publicity than the experience curve and its companion, market share. The notion underlying the theory is that people (businesses) doing something repeatedly should get better at doing it–better in an efficiency sense. For example, work hours per unit of production and, hence, labor costs per unit, should decrease in a fairly predictable manner as the volume of production accumulates. Other costs may decrease also. Researchers have documented the cost histories of a variety of products–from semiconductors to vacuum cleaners. Their bottom line would be something like this:

Unit cost is a function of accumulated experience; experience is a function of sales volume; and sales volume vis-a-vis competitors equates to market share. Therefore, the company with the highest market share should have the lowest costs and should generate the most net cash per sales dollar. In short, cash flow is a direct function of market share, and gaining and / or holding a superior market share position relative to competitors is a strategically desirable thing to do.

This concept is the basis for a continuing, keen interest in market share as a critical indicator of how a planning unit is doing at a point in time. As indicated earlier in this book, there are many fine companies today that place an extremely high priority on market share. Of course, games can be played in the measurement of market share. Your share of market depends on how you define the market. What is Porsche's market share? Or Mack Truck's? It depends. Porsche's share of the total car market is a small number. Its share of the high-price, high performance, two-seater market is a much larger number. So, market share, like any of the techniques, has its limitations. But like ROI and PLC, share can be a useful filter for straining information about the planning units of an emerging company.

Market share lends itself well to combinations with other quantitative factors important in the world of business. The most well-known combination is probably the four-cell matrix popularized by some of the leading strategy consulting firms established in recent years.

MARKET SHARE

A planning unit operating in a market with a high growth rate and which also enjoys a high market share compared to its competitors falls in the upper, left quadrant–the corner of **Stars**. It is a market leader in a high growth situation. Great! Stars may be net users of cash or they may generate excess cash, usually the former.

Cash Cows planning units are usually Stars that have moved to maturity in their PLCs. Cows operate with a high share in a market where the growth rate (activity) has declined. In effect, Cash Cows are fallen Stars! In theory, Cows should generate net cash for use elsewhere in the business.

Planning units in the **Dogs** (unfortunate label) quadrant operate in a low-growth-rate market and have a low market share to boot. Dog planning units are at the top of the list for de-investment in order to focus a business on other units in more attractive situations.

Question Marks are planning units with weak competitive positions in hot markets. In the course of a serious planning effort, presumably some of the question mark units will be selected for investment in order to strengthen their positions. Other question mark units will be pruned to free up resources for the keepers to use.

This technique is easy to understand in concept but sometimes hard to use. For example, it is very difficult to accurately determine either relative market shares or projected market growth rates for planning units in embryonic industries. With this caveat, however, this particular two-factor analysis has a great deal of merit in raising the quality of thinking and discussion about strategic matters. Here is how it can work. Suppose that after some months of intensive research by their respective planning teams, the planning units of four unrelated companies fall out as follows:

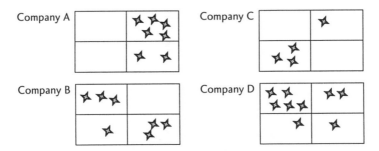

Please assume that in each of the four companies, the planning team feels that the data behind its particular matrix is reasonably representative of the reality of the operating environment. Also assume that the builders in each company wish to make practical use of their investment in planning. They want to see analysis lead to action. Below are some possible discussion issues suggested by the findings.

Company A Issues

1. Do we have enough cash to invest to move one (or more) of the Question Mark units to the left, i.e. to build it, improve its market share?

2. Can one or both of the Dog units be restarted? Or should one or both be sold or liquidated?

3. Do we have internal blockages (organization design, processes, people) that prevent us from building strong market positions in attractive markets? For example, do we have weak marketing? Are our expectations (regarding market position) vague?

Company B Issues

1. How reliable is the cash from the single Cash Cow unit? (Often on these four-cell charts the planning units are shown as circles with areas proportional to the sales volumes or cash contributions of the units.)

2. How long will the Stars keep shining, i.e. what is the time dimension of their projected PLCs? Are the Stars currently net cash users or suppliers? At what point in time will the various Star units become net cash generators?

3. Do we need to consider acquisitions or to beef up our R&D effort in order to develop some Question Mark units–potential future Stars?

4. Why do we have so many Dog units...and what is to be done with each of them?

Company C Issues

1. Is the projected, combined performance of our existing planning units compatible with our objectives?

2. How big is the potential of our one Question Mark unit, and what will it take for it to achieve a strong position over the next few years?

3. Are we short on innovation, new ideas? Are we too conservative?

Company D Issues

1. Are we giving adequate attention to projecting and monitoring future cash needs? Or, put another way, is our Cash Cow unit sufficiently large and healthy to support all our Stars and the development of at least one of our two Question Marks?
2. Are we developing a pool of talent compatible with the days ahead when some of our Stars will need to be managed for cash generation rather than growth?
3. Do we need more Question Marks in our portfolio? If so, shall we pursue them internally (R&D) or externally (via acquisition, joint ventures, alliances)?

These are the kind of pointed discussion questions that can be generated in a systematic planning process, one that makes use of one or more planning techniques to locate and compare the parts of a business. Two-factor techniques tend to stretch thinking along more dimensions than do single-factor techniques.

9
Hierarchy of Planning Techniques
Part III

"With a new focus on the service side of the business, Roberts has brought salad days back to RadioShack."
- Business Week

Multiple Factor Matrix

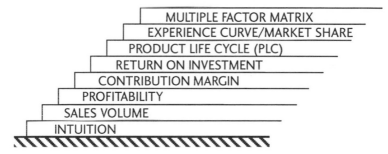

At the top step of this Hierarchy of Planning Techniques is a final technique, the Multiple Factor Matrix. In it the limits of single- and two-factor analyses are replaced by the complexity of trying to take into account more of the reality of the messy world of business. In the next diagram, the horizontal axis is labeled **Competitive Position**–a term that includes, but is broader than, simple market share. The vertical axis is **Market Attractiveness**–a term that usually includes, but is more comprehensive than, market growth rate. And the actual components of these two measuring sticks is limited only by the imagination, time, and money of the planning team.

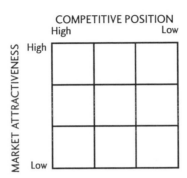

Multiple Factor Matrix

Below are the components used by the planning team in one medium-technology, emerging company to develop a map of the company.

COMPETITIVE POSITION
Marketing & Sales Issues
    Current Share: What is the unit's current position in relation to those of its active competitors?
    Reputation with Customers: How is the unit perceived and received?
    People: What is the breadth and depth of ability, i.e. how do the marketing & sales people compare to those in other companies in the industry?
    Market Knowledge: How well does unit management understand the unit's customers?

Manufacturing Issues

Value Added: How much does the unit add to its raw materials?

Cost Competitiveness: What is the unit's track record on improvements compared to competitors?

Employee Relations: What is the unit's turnover? Grievance record? Safety record?

Control Systems: Can unit management predict results (shipments, costs, etc.) with confidence?

Vendor Relations: Are key resources reliable, cooperative?

Technical Competence

People: What is the breadth and depth of talent compared to competitors?

Innovation: What has been the return on the investment in R&D over the past three years? For example, what percent of sales comes from new products now vs. four years ago?

Products

Quality: How do customers rank the unit's products compared to those of the competition?

Features: What are the distinguishing, competitive advantages of the unit's products?

Product Life Cycle: What is the risk of product obsolescence or market maturity?

Product Line: How comprehensive are the offerings by the unit compared to offerings by competitors?

Planning Unit Management

Predictability: How reliable is the management in meeting its commitments compared to the performance of competitors' management teams?

Competence: To what extent does the unit's team have proven performance in all necessary functions?

Stability and Depth: To what extent does the unit appear to have managerial reserves?

Flexibility: How well does the unit management anticipate and accommodate change?

Innovation/Productivity: What is the track record for fresh ideas over the past three years?

Unit Competitive Performance

Sales Growth: Unit sales vs. plans made vs. performance of competitors?

Earnings Growth: Unit's earnings vs. plans made vs. performance of competitors?

ROI: How well does the unit utilize its resources vs. performance of competitors?

This is a long list; the answers require a lot of work. But with the answers in hand, a planning team has a broad assessment of the competitive positions of its units. Overall, this multi-factor matrix approach requires a synthesis of two kinds of information. First, there are comparisons of the units to competitors. Such comparisons may be made on the basis of hard data, best guesses by the experienced people involved, or, most likely, a combination of the two. Second, as a practical matter, there are comparisons of a given unit to other units within the company. For example, under the category of Planning Unit Management, any unit under consideration is going to be measured against the other planning units in the business. When the planning is done, *focusing your business requires that you pick and choose among what you have.* The purpose of looking at the competitive position of each planning unit in a number of ways is to identify the strongest planning units for use in building the business.

Whereas the information on competitive position reflects both external and internal comparisons and sources, the information needed about market attractiveness comes almost solely from the field. The questions related to this dimension determine the relative merit of the various markets served, or potentially served, by the various planning units.

MARKET ATTRACTIVENESS

Total Dollars: How much money is being spent by the planning unit's natural customer base? In short, is the market a big "playing field" or a small one?

Rate of Growth: At what pace will the total dollars being spent be spent in the future?

Return on Sales: In the past, what have participants in this market earned on their sales to the customer base? Is anyone making money!?

Return on Investment: In the past, what have participants earned on the funds they have invested in this market? Is anyone making a solid return on their investment?

Ease of Entry: How easy is it for new competitors to enter into the subject market? Are there significant barriers—patents, laws, etc.?

Selling Costs: What does it take to reach the key buying influences?

Credit Worthiness: Do customers in this market pay their bills?

Strength of Competitors: How dominant—financial and marketing capabilities—are the major competitors in this market? (Is the planning unit an ant among elephants...or vice versa?)

Government Involvement: To what extent are government agencies interested and active in this market? Is this good news or bad...or neutral?

Reaction Time: In the past, how quickly do participants—customers and competitors—in this market react to innovations, change?

Vulnerability: To what extent is the market susceptible to technical or legislative obsolescence, interest rate fluctuations, weather, war or political upheaval, or other special events?

These two lists are not meant to be exhaustive, the last word. They are representative; they worked well for one emerging company. With answers to the questions on both lists, the planning team was in a position to assess the relative merits of its planning units enroute to focusing the business.

To aid the process of picking and choosing, the answers to all the questions above can be quantified. This is done by allowing, say, ten points for each answer. For example, if the answer to a given question for given unit is extremely strong, give the unit nine or ten points. Give it five for a so-so answer and one or two points if the unit is weak in the subject. If you really want to get fancy, you can weight the questions on each axis. In one way or another, it is possible to end up with numerical coordinates for each planning unit, one number for Competitive Position and one for Market Attractiveness. These coordinates can then be used to plot the positions of the units on a multiple-factor matrix for discussion purposes.

This whole exercise is not meant to be high science. It is an attempt to tease out the buried assumptions and opinions and facts key people have about the various parts of a given business. The hypothetical example shown at the top of the next page contains six planning units plotted with circles proportional in area to their sales volumes.

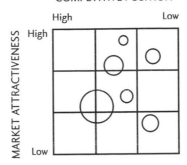

What does a planning team have when it finally gets such a matrix in front of it? Assuming that there has probably been 1) a lengthy period of serious homework, 2) a healthy portion of heated discussion enroute to a consensus about the questions and any weighting to be used, and 3) differences of opinion on the points assigned to each planning unit, then the team has a comprehensive, composite picture of how the various parts of the enterprise relate to one another and to the world outside. The picture isn't perfect, but it puts judgments out in the open where they can be scrutinized. The multiple factor matrix, just as the other techniques in the planning hierarchy, can provide business builders with a basis for decisions about where best to allocate resources—primarily talent and cash—in the future. This is the purpose of strategic planning.

Given a multiple factor matrix, legitimate questions are bound to arise:
1. Is/was the choice we made of planning units correct? Did they lend themselves to data collection and analysis? Are they usefully comparable to one another? Are they indigenous/organic to our business?
2. Is the data we used valid? Are we dealing with the reality of our operating environment?

3. Do we believe the picture we see? Is it a fair represen-
   tation of what is?
4. If this picture is "true enough," what next?

There is a solid base of experience in the use of multiple factor matrixes. Some users have produced what
they dub the Build, Hold, Harvest map. These three labels denote strategic assignments enroute to focusing a
given business, i.e. positioning it at the crossroads of
opportunity and capability.

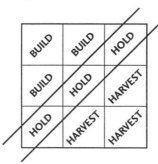

The diagonal lines divide the array of planning units
into three classes. The divisions are arrived at somewhat arbitrarily. For example, they might be arrived at
by simply dividing all the planning units into thirds.
Other times natural divisions appear. The end result,
however, is that a Build strategic assignment suggests
an aggressive expansion of the unit's presence in the
marketplace.

To **BUILD**, most likely, means to move out along one
of the pathways outlined in Chapter 4. Representative
operating moves for Build units include:
- Adding to marketing and sales staffs.
- Pricing aggressively.
- Aggressive use of Internet and other newer
  mediums for communication.

- Accelerate product development & introductions.
- Expand and/or develop management team.
- Explore acquisition of smaller competitors.
- Expand capacity.
- Forge alliances to broaden market reach, e.g., internationally.

Such moves will, of course, require investment. Most likely Build planning units will have a negative short-term cash flow. Therefore, they may provide at least a short-term drag on earnings and ROI. Such a performance penalty may be acceptable if it is part of an overall plan for pursuing the expectations of the enterprise.

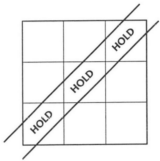

A **HOLD** strategic assignment suggests that the current position in the marketplace will be maintained *vis-a-vis* competition. Whether the market is growing or shrinking, the task is for the planning unit to remain where it is. This type of assignment is roughly comparable to being a productive Cash Cow in the simpler, two-factor matrix. Representative operating moves for Hold planning units include:

- Cultivate key customers (opinion leaders) in chosen segments carefully.
- Develop product and product-line extensions selectively.

- Integrate vertically or develop fresh initiatives with vendors to become or remain a low-cost producer.
- Initiate value engineering and productivity programs.
- Control working capital tightly.
- Confuse major competitors by using marketing feints and tactics, e.g., pre-announce new products or facilities.
- Refine mission and vision elements of the expectations pyramid (see Chapter 12) for the business.

Units in the HOLD class usually constitute the backbone of a business. They are, normally, strong earnings producers–the driving forces behind the successful emergence of a company to date.

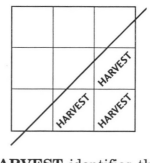

The term **HARVEST** identifies the third class. A Harvest strategic assignment suggests a controlled loss of competitive position during which major amounts of cash are released for use elsewhere in the enterprise. In short, it means that the builders of the business extract resources from a unit. They harvest it. This is the bottom line of focusing your business, of strategic planning: Reallocating cash and people.

Appropriate operating moves that might be integrated into the annual plans of planning units with a

Harvest assignment include:
- Raise prices.
- Avoid investment in new equipment and/or facilities.
- Consolidate/rationalize facilities.
- Reduce sales, marketing, R&D, management expenses.
- Seek buyers for parts or all of the unit.
- Trim inventories and services.
- Alter the composition of the management team and incentives to reflect the winding-down nature of the assignment.

Harvesting is often tough to do in an emerging company. First there is the decision hurdle. It is harder to do surgery based on planning than to do it under emergency conditions. Second there is plan execution. Many growth company people are builders by nature; de-construction is an unnatural act. Then, too, it is just plain difficult to back away from a historical piece of the business that has merely lost its luster when compared with other opportunities at hand. Leadership is required.

With reference precisely to units in the Harvest class, Jack Welch, the CEO of GE, framed his marching orders this way: "Fix, close, or sell." In certain circumstances, Welch (and others) have allowed some time for unit leaders to "fix" their businesses, i.e., to find a way to boost them to the Hold or even the Build classes.

J.T. Battenberg III, the head of GM's huge Delphi business (auto parts), is credited with rejuvenating Delphi which was once a Harvest-class unit. According to the *Wall Street Journal:*

> *After four years of restructuring, Delphi is profitable and has turned into a formidable competitor, aggressively chasing business outside GM and outside the U.S., particularly in Asia. Delphi, once a candidate for harvesting, is now a build.*[14]

Build, Hold, Harvest are arbitrary designations. The idea is to come up with strategic assignments for the various parts of the business. The sum of the assignments reflects the longer-term direction in which the total enterprise will be built. The multiple factor matrix provides a methodology to synthesize other techniques and judgment calls into a single picture that can help in sorting through a business. If you decide to concentrate–focus–on some of the parts of the picture, other parts are going to disappear from view. Ideally, this is done systematically, not precipitously. Diagonal lines are not a necessity. Whatever works! The idea is to come up with strategic assignments for the portfolio of parts, the sum of which produces a company that lasts.

10
The Planning Process

"None of us is as smart as all of us."
- Phil Condit, Boeing

The previous three chapters provided the technical underpinning for sorting through the parts of a business in pursuit of focus. This chapter is the philosophical heart of the book. In the fifteen or twenty years that strategic planning has been creeping onto the scene, several lessons have become clear. They are summarized as follows:

*Strategic planning is an **operating management activity** centered on getting **the right people, agenda, and information** together on a **timely schedule** in order to make **decisions that commit cash and people to marketplace positioning assignments extending beyond the current operating cycle**.*

Please consider the lessons embodied above:

"... operating management activity ...."

As suggested in an earlier chapter, in the world of business a large percentage of all strategic plans end up languishing in three-ring binders. They were read, discussed, and then forgotten. There was feeble implementation and, therefore, no significant payoff. None of the products or markets or activities of the burgeoning companies were pruned back due to planning. Except for a few obvious losers, all of the initiatives of the past were left in place. Much of the time the enterprises continued to grow contentedly until...usually until unexpected slowdowns in performance force some level of discipline on the leadership.

What is the practical alternative to this approach? How can implementation be woven tightly into the fabric of a plan from the first day of planning? A big part of the answer is: The planners must be the same people who will be responsible for carrying out the plan. The planning team must be the operating team.

Following are three common mistakes made by well-meaning people intent on focusing their businesses.

Excessive Reliance on a Planning Staff

A well-known, medium-sized, consumer-products company got the strategy bug. The president hired a very creative, aggressive, senior manager away from a larger company in a related field. She became the vice-president of planning. Three years and two big plans later, the new executive was released and the position was eliminated. The consensus of the senior people was this: Although the many hours spent planning were interesting, albeit expensive, the chief planner was never really able to design a comprehensive program that set well with a healthy cross-section of the management.

There is a big difference between a planning director that sees him- or herself as *the* architect of a company plan and one that sees himself or herself as a processor, catalyzer, or facilitator. In building a company, there is a great deal of *very* important support work that an effective planner or staff can do. Most of the planning techniques in the hierarchy require data other than what is routinely generated internally. The data must be dug up, massaged, and put into forms useful for review and discussion. And there is plenty of opportunity for an effective planner to nudge plans in directions suggested by his or her professional expertise. However, the moment operating people are off the hook because a strategic plan has become the planner's plan, the probability of implementation and payoff dives.

Consultants

An old-line northeastern company hired a consulting firm to develop a long-range plan. The consultants did a thorough job of analyzing the market, internal costs, and competition. They developed a comprehensive picture of the relative strengths and weaknesses of the company, and they accurately identified a major gap between where the company was likely to be in five years and where a company that kept up with industry norms should be in terms of performance. The team did a limited, multiple factor matrix analysis of the business using the operating divisions as the planning units. The team then presented its recommendations which included harvesting the oldest part of the business on one hand and moving into related, fast-food retailing on the other. The consultants had carefully pre-sold their ideas to most of the key people on an individual basis. However, when the senior people met together to receive the final report, they rejected 80% of the recommendations on the spot as unrealistic and not in keeping with the traditions of the company.

As in the case of a planning staff, an outside and/or inside consulting team can serve as a major and cost-effective supporting mechanism to operating management. But any plan must end up as the plan *of* the operating management, not a plan *for* it. It is a delicate difference.

Board of Directors

Boards are very much in the spotlight today, especially given the turmoil at the top of corporate icons like GM, IBM, Westinghouse, and ADM. Much of the press coverage suggests that corporations ought to increase the ratio of outsiders to insiders. Virtually all of the coverage favors expanding the roles played by boards in the affairs of the company. "Expanded oversight" is the phrase regularly used. As spelled out in Chapter 2, much of the interest in increasing the percentage of outsiders on the board is associated with the emergence of nonmarket issues as areas of corporate responsibility. *Wisdom about nonmarket matters, however, does not necessarily qualify board members to contribute usefully to the development of strategic plans.* When the depth of thinking required to define planning units and develop doable scenarios for a fast-moving, emerging company is considered, the limitations of board members who spend perhaps ten days a year devoted to the enterprise become evident. This is not an argument against outsiders; it is a plea for more creative thinking about the composition and use of boards in a emerging company. Knowledgeable directors can be an extremely valuable element in the process of building a company that lasts.

Here is one model that speaks to this issue. Texas Instruments, a company that has emerged very nicely, heavily involves its outside board members in various aspects of the company at a rate exceeding thirty days a year. The familiarity with TI that comes from this extended participation enhances the ability of the directors to contribute to the strategic issues confronting the company. The ability and willingness to participate at least thirty days a year is part of the criteria for board membership at TI. Were this kind of a requirement used more broadly in the business community, it would eliminate many of the "trophy" kind of directors who spend a great deal of time flitting from company to company but who know each company only superficially.

To conclude this first point about the strategic planning process: Plan implementation is greatly enhanced when at least the operating managers of a business are at the center of the entire process.

"...the right people, agenda, and information..."

The word "process" suggests a particular method of doing something. A process generally involves a number of steps done sequentially, and often teamwork is an important part of making a process productive. Most business builders favor teamwork, and well they should. As authors Katzenbach and Smith put it:

> *Teamwork represents a set of values that encourage listening and responding constructively to views expressed by others, giving others the benefit of the doubt, providing support, and recognizing the interests and achievements of others. Such values help teams perform, and they also promote individual performance as well as the performance of the entire organization.*[15]

Off and on throughout this book the term, planning *team*, has been used. *Not all groupings of people are teams.* Some are merely groups–formations–of people! There is a difference. Following are some common formations to use with caution, if at all:

Planning Task Forces or Committees

These are typically set up on *ad hoc* basis. Members of such work groups often have difficulty giving enough time and energy to planning to generate a solid blueprint for building the business. Members also tend to attend the get-togethers to represent their home departments. They become couriers, representatives. Katzenbach & Smith spell out the typical characteristics of working groups (as opposed to teams) in their *Harvard Business Review* article, "The Discipline of Teams." The characteristics, paraphrased, are:

Working Groups have...
– A strong, clearly focused leader
– Individual accountability
– A purpose the same as that of the larger unit
– Individual work products
– Efficient meetings
– Indirect measures of effectiveness
– Discussions, decisions, and delegation

The authors contrast the above with the typical characteristics (paraphrased) of true teams:

Teams have...
– Shared leadership roles
– Individual *and* mutual accountability
– A team purpose the team itself will deliver
– Collective work products
– Open-ended discussion+active problem solving
– Performance measures based on work products
– Real work and decision-making done together

The complete article, "The Discipline of Teams," is included as Reading II in this book.

Task Forces and Committees may be teams. Then again, they may not.

Management Retreats

It is a very tempting prospect. The hard-driving senior people of a fast-growing company adjourn from the hustle and bustle and go to the woods or beach for a few days where lofty thoughts and dreams for the future can soar without the pressure of now. Where better to achieve focus? There are several drawbacks in this scheme, however, in addition to the onetime nature of the retreat. The biggest one is that most likely all the right people will not be present. The right people for an effective planning process vary over time as different planning units and different issues—competitive position, market attractiveness, for instance—are aired. If the right people are not present, neither will be the right information.

> The management team of a very dynamic San Francisco company removed itself to Pebble Beach for a five-day session focused on a three-year plan. The team was accompanied by several consultants and staff people who assisted the CEO and others throughout the week. There was a great deal of discussion in and out of the meeting rooms, and some tentative conclusions were reached regarding future directions. But the spirit of the meeting was best expressed by a senior vice-president who, at the finish of the last scheduled meeting, rose from his place at the green, felt-covered table, rubbed his hands together, and exclaimed with a big smile, "Great! Now let's get back to work!"

Another drawback to retreating to plan is that, by design, key people are removed from the day-to-day realities of the business. This positioning of the process outside the mainstream of the business can give it an unreal or academic aura. Being academic does not augur well for implementation! Does this mean there is no place for offsite meetings in the total scheme of things? Of course not. Properly done, offsites can provide the best possible forum for boosting the acceptance of plans. Properly done. An article by your author on the subject of management meetings, "Are You Walkin' What You're Talkin'" is included as Reading III. [16] But retreats have real limitations in a planning effort to focus a business.

"...a timely schedule..."

There are two major mistakes to avoid concerning timing. The first has already been discussed—namely, a once-a-year strategic planning retreat. The major change that usually accompanies honest focusing has to be cultivated and grown throughout the year. The second mistake is to couple a strategic planning effort to budgeting for the next fiscal year. Such coupling is common. It has at least two major drawbacks:

1. Coupling encourages the extrapolation of current thinking. What do you do when you are rushed—as you always are—to prepare a budget? You make incremental changes at the margin, i.e. you avoid big breaks with tradition. It takes time to think big! When strategic matters are mixed up with tactical ones, what is important is most often elbowed aside by what is urgent.

2. Trade-off decisions about strategic assignments for various planning units will be tainted by the budget battle for dollars and/or current performance concerns. Budgeting should be one of the last steps in an effective longer-range planning sequence.

In time, the annual calendar for an emerging company should provide a smooth sequence that covers both a review of strategic matters and planning for the coming year. Following are the highlights of such a sequence. The sequence shown assumes there is at least general agreement on the expectations, including objectives, for the enterprise.

1. Define the planning units.

2. Prepare a business position audit of each planning unit. It should include the following: historic sales, earnings, growth rate, and technology-trend information; current status of market share and other factors deemed important by the planning team; outlook to the planning horizon including expected moves by competitors and government agencies; viable, longer-range scenarios for the unit (what *could* be done with it) and the projected costs and returns for each scenario.

3. Review the audit of each planning unit. In a series of semiformal meetings, the planning team should review the audits. As a result of the discussions, a consensus should be reached about where each unit stands competitively now and the attractiveness of the market(s) served. Consensus should be sought about the realistic, possible scenarios for the future. (What could or will the unit become if ...?)

At this point it is important to note that new audits will *not* be prepared every year. It is necessary to develop an initial, in-depth point of view about each planning unit, one based on sound data collection, analysis, and thinking. Once a point of view is in hand, however, future planning cycles will require only updating or confirming the positions of the units.

4. Relate the planning units to one another to form a composite view of the enterprise. The planning techniques in the upper end of the planning hierarchy can be useful at this point. By way of review, the matrix shown at the top of the next page is one framework for looking at a whole enterprise.

5. Analyze the portfolio of units. Decide on the strategic assignments for the various units, for example, Build, Hold, Harvest. This is the heart of focusing your business. Here is where you must pick, choose, prune, cut away the old to make way for the new. Note: Decisions made at this step may have important implications to the overall organization design of the enterprise as well as to many of its key processes such as compensation, hiring, and so on. (More on this in Chapter 15.)

6. Prepare a comprehensive plan for each unit, based on its strategic assignment. Such a plan should be the blueprint for achieving specified objectives. In effect, it is a business plan covering markets, facilities, people, cash projections, etc. Ideally it will revolve around a decision on strategy including the choice for a sustainable competitive advantage—product superiority, applications expertise, convenience—as well as a pathway for growth—home base, product line expansion, etc.

7. Review unit plans. Now, in a series of semiformal meetings, the senior building team should review the detailed plans submitted by the people responsible for the units. Revisions based on resource availability and other factors can be made as appropriate.

The compilation of the unit's plans now becomes the master plan for the entire enterprise unless there are new areas of activity to be pursued outside the existing planning-unit structure. This plan, which started with audits of the planning units, should be a living document, a baseline against which subsequent annual operating details can be formulated and measured. The sum of the unit plans is the road map to the future. This map should point the way to changes in the company structure, job assignments for key people, and even needed adjustments to the culture of the company. See Chapter 15 for more on the implications of planning.

8. Prepare, review, and adopt annual operating plans. This step can now become an upgraded or broadened version of the usual budgeting process. The added ingredient is the presence of a strategic plan that serves as a guideline to the budget details.

9. Conduct regular reviews. Here builders track how well units are doing in terms of performance compared to the adopted operating plans.

10. Repeat steps 1-9 in subsequent time periods. As experience dictates, redefine the planning units in step 1, redo the audits of step 2, etc.

These ten steps are a general guideline. A balanced, informed point of view has to be formed by the planning team about each of the pieces that form the jigsaw puzzle that is the company. The pieces need to be sorted through systematically and compared. Decisions need to be reached about strategic assignments. Most emerging companies have finite resources so not every piece can be a Build. A portfolio of assignments is more realistic. Some pieces of the business must generate net cash, for example, to fund the growth of other pieces.

The process of analysis and reaching decisions is neither as rational nor as lockstep as it appears here in print. There is and will be a significant portion of muddling through. But the fact that muddling occurs does not negate the usefulness of a disciplined process in a complex, emerging company.

"...decisions that commit cash and people to marketplace positioning assignments extending beyond the current operating cycle...".

One excellent test question that helps evaluate the realness of any strategic planning effort in an emerging company is this:

Was a decision made to stop doing anything?

If the answer is no, chances are the planning process or effort was ineffectual. There is no more focus at the end than there was at the beginning! Particularly in the first few cycles of planning, emerging companies almost always need to discard some of their existing baggage to release resources for use elsewhere. This "did we stop doing anything" test is a handy one.

Another test question is this:

Is available money and talent actually channeled into chosen areas of opportunity?

If the answer is no, it means the resources of the enterprise will be going where they have historically gone regardless of the realities of the operating environment, including the current strengths and weaknesses of the enterprise.

Strategic planning is really a managing process to focus your business in the face of debilitating complexity. There was a time when strategic planning was a luxury. Today it is a necessity for business builders in emerging companies.

11
Summary
Chapters 6-10

*"A wise person will hear and increase
in understanding."*
- Proverbs 1:5

When you focus a camera, you hone in on some parts of the total scene captured by the lens and let the rest of the parts become blurred. You concentrate your attention and, in time, the attention of others who view the finished print or slide. When you focus your business at a certain point in time, you hone in on some of its parts at the expense of other parts. You pick the ones which will give you the best shot at reaching your expectations. Focusing can be done by gut feel, by looking at the numbers, sometimes by following the crowd, or via strategic planning–a process. Chapters 6-10 were about strategic planning.

As a company succeeds it usually becomes larger and more complex. Because of this, the price tag on trial-and-error decisions creeps up. So does the psychological cost of failure. With success, egos balloon and grow tender. With success, even greater things become possible. However, focusing on them is difficult because there is so much to do, i.e. there is more in the picture than before. Most any team of people that has brought its enterprise through the survival stage can do effective planning...if they get around to it.

The organic parts–building blocks–of the business need to be identified. *The choice of planning units affects the outcome of the planning effort.* Then a point of view needs to be formulated about each part. Where does it stand in relation to its competition? *Businesses compete against one another, not against some absolute standard.* What are the realities of the marketplace served? *Identifying and dealing with reality is the continuing task of business leadership.* Finally, all the units need to be compared one to another in search of a combination of initiatives that balances risks, potential outcomes, and the pursuit of expectations for the enterprise.

There are a variety of techniques that can be used to facilitate the search, but the real heart of the matter is a *process* that meshes the right people, agenda, and information together. The product of the process is a set of assignments to which the people of the enterprise can respond. If a shop foreman or salesperson or operations supervisor doesn't understand the assignment well, chances are it will not be carried out with vigor, if at all.

Regardless of its quality, there is a certain attraction to a completed plan. The black-and-white sureness of the printed pages, the visual harmony of the pie charts, matrixes, and flow diagrams, and the optimism inherent in all the projections speak to the crying need for order in the sea of chaos upon which most emerging companies float. But most business veterans know that the usual three-ring binders full of rationality are an illusion–a necessary illusion, perhaps–but an illusion nonetheless. *The planning results that are most important are the ones implanted in the minds of the participants in the process, not the results on the pages in the binders.*

The process should produce a relatively high degree of enlightened consistency in the attitudes, outlooks, intentions, and ultimately, the behavior of the pacesetters of the enterprise. Focusing your business via effective planning is an integral part of being on the offensive against your competitors.

Preview
Chapters 12-15

Plan execution has many requirements because it must take place in the rough-and-tumble, boisterous world of business where, daily, great names fall from grace and upstarts make headlines. Execution must be timely since the scene changes quickly. It must reflect a goodly amount of self-reliance because there are so many uncontrollables. It must lead to regular, small victories in order to inspire confidence in its validity. And it must be true to a plan which, hopefully, points the way toward an attractive intersection of opportunity and capability.

The chapters that follow introduce the rest of the story on focusing your business through strategic planning. Plans are means to an end. Plans need to be generated in the context of expectations, and plans should reflect due consideration of opportunities and capabilities, strengths and weaknesses. Builders of businesses need to take the pulse of their organizations prior to choosing a pathway to follow and perhaps along the way as well. Finally, business builders vitally need perspective on "managing" work and the ways in which it differs from "doing" work. Both kinds of work are required to build a business.

12
Setting
Expectations

"We are at the beginning of another great journey."
 - Bill Gates, Microsoft

Emerging companies are wonderful places for people to reach unexpected levels of achievement–individually and as part of the total enterprise. One underlying theme of this book is that people tend to rise to meet expectations. But to do this, people must know what the expectations are! Unknown, expectations have little utility. To review the groundwork laid in Chapter 2, in a business setting expectations come in three levels of abstraction. Think of them as the parts of the Expectations Pyramid.

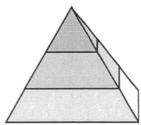

Expectations Pyramid

At the apex are visions, the most abstract level of expectations. Ideally, visions are *inspirational* to the people who share them. In the middle of the pyramid are missions. They are less abstract, more specific, and typically longer statements than visions. Effective missions are *educational* for those involved. Like visions, missions are a form of expectations. At the base of the pyramid are objectives which are individual building blocks supporting the pursuit of the mission and vision. Objectives are *operational*–measurable, dated, end results to be achieved. Visions are rare in emerging companies. Missions are found more frequently. Objectives are the minimum form of expectations required to focus your business. Here, paraphrased, is the way Bob Noyce, a cofounder of Intel put it when he was the vice-chairman:

> *In a small organization there's enough communication so that the objectives are very clearly defined. So our organization was sharply focused through the first couple of years. Then we ran out of collective experience. Only one member of the board had worked for a company larger than Intel. We had to plow new ground in order to keep focused.*[6]

Since objectives and MBO were covered in Chapter 2, this chapter is mostly about visions and missions. Where do they fit into the work of focusing your business? Do you need all three–objectives, a mission, and a vision? Or just one or two?

Visions

Many people feel vision statements are bunk, or at best, pretty wall paper. You can make up your own mind on this. Following are a few examples of visions at work and the possible benefits they provide.

Visions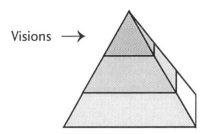

One of the leading construction firms in the United States has a vision. The people in the firm live by this statement. We will work "...to improve the standard of living and quality of life, worldwide." If you were a top engineer just graduating from college and you had some reasons to believe this vision was for real, would you tilt toward joining the company? Sometimes visions can help attract and keep good people.

Here is another example: "We are in the business of preserving and improving human life." This vision is central to being a part of the Merck pharmaceutical company, a model enterprise in many ways for decades. Merck executives and scientists believe the vision is a positive force in the life of the company.

If you are on the varsity team at Boeing, it is likely that some part of you yearns to be "...on the leading edge of aeronautics." It is said that one has to want to eat, breathe, and sleep aviation to feel comfortable at Boeing, and that this vision serves as a magnet to many people in this now-giant enterprise which must continually re-invent itself as its industry evolves.

Following are two more visions from respected names homebased on opposite sides of the world: "We will contribute to the welfare of society by responding to contemporary needs through excellent technology and creativity." ...and... "We will be the driving force in the development, manufacture, marketing, and servicing of quality vehicles in the best European tradition." The first is from Mitsubishi; the second from Volkswagen. Note how each statement emphasizes different behavior–technology and creativity in one case, quality in the other. Different visions.

In your author's study of visions, there seem to be five common denominators that characterize *productive* vision statements, i.e., ones that honestly influence behavior on a continuing basis. Such visions are:

• **Anchored in a big, external reality.** Corporations are creations of society and fairly recent creations at that. Over the longer run, companies exist to serve society. While providing jobs and creating shareholder wealth are examples of such services, these services to internal constituencies may not be enough to fully energize all the people involved as an emerging company increases in size and complexity. Something more may be required, a higher calling. A vision can provide this.

• **Indigenous.** A particular vision only needs to work and survive in one place, in the organization where it was born. A vision is a native; it is homegrown. It doesn't matter what you think about any of the visions mentioned above since you are not a part of Merck or Boeing or Mitsubishi or Volkswagen. You are in some other place.

• **Timeless.** A vision for a company provides the rationale for its continuing existence, the justification for a long life for the enterprise itself. A viable vision transcends products and facilities, good leadership and bad, changes in strategy, downsizing, rightsizing, growth, democrats and republicans, upheavals of all sorts. A useful vision is a beacon lighting the way regardless of the weather.

• **Trackable in the real world, over time.** You can tell if you are on course. The most common tracking metrics are those having to do with customers and sales volume and profitability and share of market and returns on assets. A business that is pursuing a useful vision gets feedback automatically. Visions are not dreams. Visions are high expectations toward which people work. But people need feedback, "the breakfast of champions," as author Ken Blanchard terms it in his book, *The One Minute Manager.*[17]

• **Simple.** The examples above as well as other research on the subject suggests that productive visions are simple. Their lucidness is often disarming, but short, abstract statements *can* actually drive behavior in growing companies. Such statements can also serve as tiebreakers when questions of direction or focus or proper conduct arise. When one examines the list of companies that are standing the test of time, some of them–certainly not all, but some of them–do seem to revolve around a central, organizing, living expectation which stands senior to everything else.

So, five characteristics of a vision to consider. Does going through the muddy process of sorting out a vision help a business do well over the longer haul? It may in these times which, as philosopher Joseph Campbell put it, "...every one of the great traditions is in profound disorder." A solid vision can provide a compass heading for the people who make up an organization to follow as they struggle though the ever-changing terrain that goes with the act of emerging.

Missions

Whereas visions tend to be primarily internal or private, missions are more institutional, more public. Missions typically contain a lot on who "we" will serve and how "we" will operate. In the ideal case, a mission summarizes the current framework for the pursuit of the vision of the enterprise. For example, at one fast-growing company, Scott Specialty Gases, the Mission Statement includes a short Vision followed by a Mission, Goals, and a Management Philosophy—all on one page. And spunky Heart Federal's "Constitution" covers Mission, Goals, Long-Term Corporate Strategy, Corporate Commitment, and each Individual's Commitment—all in two pages.

Missions ⟶

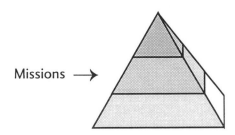

Missions usually strive to take into account the present reality and current capabilities of an enterprise. Missions are often produced by a team of people. Visions, on the other hand, tend to flow from the minds of one or a few individuals; visions are, as a rule, less democratic, you might say. A vision is enduring, timeless; but a mission should normally be altered in important ways as an organization's operating environment shifts. This is an important distinction between these two forms of expectations. *Missions need to be updated from time to time.*

If a vision is inspirational, a mission is educational. It describes the who, what, and how of a given business at a given period in time. More often than not a mission is published so it can be distributed widely in the organization and often outside, too. For example, Blue Cross-Blue Shield put its mission in its annual report to shareholders. This is not uncommon. Missions can convey a lot of information about an emerging company.

First a mission covers **who** the enterprise seeks to serve. **Who** is usually some mix of customers, employees, shareholders, people in the community, and, perhaps, society itself. Details vary, of course, but here are some examples of constituencies mentioned on some representative, emerging company mission statements.

At Basic American Foods the mission statement is called, "What We Stand For." The paragraph headings include...

     Customers
     Employees
     Community
     Shareholders.

At Johnson & Johnson the mission is called the "J&J Credo." **Who**, in the Credo, includes...

     Doctors
     Nurses
     Patients
     Suppliers
     Distributors
     Employees
     Communities
     Stockholders.

Next, a mission covers **what** which usually means the output of business. The possibilities are finite...
> Products
> Services
> Products & Services

At Ford, the output is a product, an auto or truck. At Disney, it is a service, entertainment. At Nordstrom, you get, "service above all else," but you walk away with products under your arm. The same is true at Wal-Mart. Quite a few mission statements include modifiers such as value-added or quality, as in "we will create, sell, and service quality widgets." These modifiers further refine expectations for the people of the enterprise.

A mission also covers **how.** Here are some examples. We will...
> Continually improve
> Be market-driven
> Respect individuals
> Operate as a seamless federation
> Take risks
> Be technology-driven
> Reward initiative
> Be entrepreneurial

Values often arise in connection with the **how** of mission statements. For example, the Terminal Corporation's Mission devotes almost half the statement to values such as...
> People make the difference
> Excellence in quality and service
> Profits to build the future

The how part of a mission typically spells out a code of conduct for the people of the enterprise, including the types of behavior most treasured. For example, the presence of the J&J Credo mentioned earlier is credited, in

large part, for the quick response by the Johnson &
Johnson Company in pulling all the Tylenol in the U.S.A.
off retail shelves during the Tylenol scare in 1981. It
was a $100 million recall triggered by package tamper-
ing in the Chicago area.

An effective mission spells out who, what, and how.
It usually also covers the fact that success in carrying
out the mission will be measured, in part, by the
profitability of the enterprise. For example, Mack Truck's
Mission includes the words: "...to remain competitive and
prosperous over the long term and to provide a fair return
to our shareholder." Hewlett-Packard's well-known
mission, *The H-P Way*, includes this sign post: "To achieve
sufficient profit to finance our company growth and to
provide the resources we need to achieve our other
corporate objectives." The bottom line is that mission
statements in emerging companies need to cover the
bottom line or they are dishonest.

Objectives

If, in terms of expectations, a vision is inspirational
and a mission is educational, then, objectives are operational. Few companies have a vision; some companies
have a mission; nearly all companies have objectives.
Objectives are the most tangible expression of expectations. Here are some examples of objectives. Increase sales
to $200M by the end of 1999. Raise market share by four
points next year. Reduce unit costs at least 15% within
eighteen months. Complete the annual performance reviews as scheduled. The possibilities are endless.

Objectives are results to be achieved, and sound objectives share two characteristics: they are **measurable**
and they are **dated**. The combination of measurable and
dated means progress against them is visible. You know
whether or not you are achieving the results sought.
Other people do, too.

Objectives channel attention to the point of execution where human resources are applied directly to the tasks at hand. In an era of decentralization and empowerment, complexity and speed, objectives are the day-to-day building blocks of an ongoing company. Objectives *focus* attention. Without objectives, people may well work hard, but synergism between people is difficult. Measurable, dated objectives lie near the heart of purposeful, collective effort.

Objectives $\longrightarrow$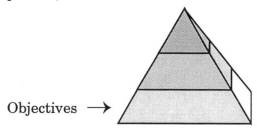

Now why should a management team go through the often troublesome process of getting objectives down on paper? Because "on paper" is commitment. And commitment makes things happen. Here is a quote by Goethe that your author saw recently in a book about climbing Mt. Everest:

Until one is committed, there is hesitancy, the chance to draw back...always ineffectiveness. Concerning all acts of initiative or creation, there is one elementary truth, the ignorance of which kills countless ideas and splendid plans: That the moment one commits oneself, then Providence moves too. All sorts of things occur to help one that would otherwise never have occurred. A whole stream of events issue from the decision, raising in one's favor all manner of incidents and meetings and material.

-Goethe

To summarize this chapter: Focusing your business via a strategic planning process requires you to aim to be some things to some people. Setting expectations is an act of deciding what things to what people. At the highest level of abstraction is vision, a succinct word picture of why the enterprise seeks to continue. A vision is, hopefully, both inspiring and enduring. At the mid-level of abstraction is mission, an educational statement about the business in the near term. A mission will usually change over time as the operating environment changes. At the lowest level are objectives, the building blocks of day-to-day management and supervision. In a successful company, objectives will be aligned with the more senior expectations of the organization.

The philosophical underpinning for this book is that people need to know what is expected of them in order to focus their efforts, and that people *do* rise to meet expectations. Expectations are like magnets; they draw people to them. They guide behavior. In a complicated, competitive world, sound expectations are an important step to cutting through the clutter and confusion. And when a group of people share the same expectations, there is an opportunity for them to pull together in the same direction.

13
Taking the Pulse of Your Organization

*"Our most important assets wear shoes
and go home at night."*

- various

Focusing your business means precisely honing in on a particular intersection of opportunity and capability. Much of this book has been about assessing the opportunity dimension. Capability was certainly a part of determining a planning unit's Competitive Position in Chapter 9. But a lot of what makes up the true capability of an emerging company has to do with intangibles such as attitude and outlook, "people things." More companies fall by the wayside because of poor plan execution than because of poor plans. Poor execution is a "people thing." The more business builders know about how their people feel about things, the smarter will be the decision-making aimed at positioning the enterprise for continuing success. One way to find out how people feel about important matters, including plans that affect them, is to ask.

Just a few years back MBWA (Management By Walking Around) was touted as the way to keep in touch as a company grew. Bill Hewlett and David Packard popularized this approach at H-P. But the plain facts are that MBWA has practical limitations in companies of any size, particularly if the physical parts of the enterprise (plants, offices, etc.) are spread around geographically. A complementary idea whose time seems to be coming is the idea of systematically surveying employees to check the pulse of the enterprise. Just as business builders need information on inventory, backlog, and cash levels, they also need regular readouts on the sentiments of the human resources of the company. Surveys are not a substitute for one-on-one contact via walking around, but they can fill out and give definition to the reality that exists.

Here is the way one emerging company executive sees the situation:

The 700 European employees of the public relations firm of Burson-Marsteller / Europe are polled monthly via the company's in-house computer system. Responses flow in via e-mail. Full survey results–typically from a surprising 85 percent of employees–materialize within 48 hours, replete with breakdowns by division, country, and seniority level. Ferdinand de Bakker, Burson Europe's chief executive and many others dismiss the idea that surveys are a form of Big Brother (watching). They see their surveys as nothing less than a new means for a democratization of the workplace. To use the jargon of the moment, they see the exercise as part of an empowerment of the workforce, a means by which employees can exert influence over their own professional destinies and those of their firms.[18]

Taking the pulse of your organization in a systematic manner is not for the fainthearted! You may receive unwelcome answers! But the potential returns for those who dare are great. Suppose you used the following short survey in your enterprise. Take it yourself first. For each statement, make a check mark (✓) at Strongly Agree, Agree, Neutral or Don't Know, Disagree, or Strongly Disagree. Then go back over the ten statements and mark Xs where you think the consolidated results would fall if all *your* key people took the survey.

SURVEY

1. Our company is well-structured to compete effectively in the markets we aim to serve between now and the year 2002.

   Strongly   Agree   Neutral or   Disagree   Strongly
   Agree   Don't Know   Disagree

   _____   _____   _____   _____   _____

2. People at all organizational levels have a clear understanding of our company's goals and objectives.

   Strongly   Agree   Neutral or   Disagree   Strongly
   Agree   Don't Know   Disagree

   _____   _____   _____   _____   _____

3. The management teams of our business units make good use of information technology to enhance responsiveness and competitiveness.

   Strongly   Agree   Neutral or   Disagree   Strongly
   Agree   Don't Know   Disagree

   _____   _____   _____   _____   _____

4. I am continually stimulated and challenged in my work in our company.

   Strongly   Agree   Neutral or   Disagree   Strongly
   Agree   Don't Know   Disagree

   _____   _____   _____   _____   _____

5. Across our company there is a high degree of accountability for achieving the plans that are made.

   Strongly   Agree   Neutral or   Disagree   Strongly
   Agree   Don't Know   Disagree

   _____   _____   _____   _____   _____

more →

6. Our strategic planning process is producing important insights and actions for the future.

Strongly Agree	Agree	Neutral or Don't Know	Disagree	Strongly Disagree
_____	_____	_____	_____	_____

7. Fear of making big mistakes does not seem to interfere with the decision-making process within our company.

Strongly Agree	Agree	Neutral or Don't Know	Disagree	Strongly Disagree
_____	_____	_____	_____	_____

8. For the most part, I know what is expected of me as I carry out my assigned responsibilities.

Strongly Agree	Agree	Neutral or Don't Know	Disagree	Strongly Disagree
_____	_____	_____	_____	_____

9. We have about the right balance between centralization and decentralization to be very competitive.

Strongly Agree	Agree	Neutral or Don't Know	Disagree	Strongly Disagree
_____	_____	_____	_____	_____

10. We are well positioned to be an effective competitor in the years ahead.

Strongly Agree	Agree	Neutral or Don't Know	Disagree	Strongly Disagree
_____	_____	_____	_____	_____

The subjects above tend to be big-picture issues; they relate to the strategic intent and degree of focus in a business. In practice, the statements can be about anything. The answers to the specific statements above, however, have proven helpful in getting companies into focus. Presumably the key people in an emerging company should be reasonably in agreement with and supportive of what is being done on the subjects covered in the ten statements. Otherwise, debilitating conflict, half-heartedness, buck passing, second guessing, turf wars, and all manner of side effects are likely to render the enterprise ineffective in executing plans. This is true regardless of how well such plans are anchored in the intricacies of the marketplace.

Can surveys such as this sample contribute meaningfully to the assessment of capability by those who have the primary responsibility for building a given business? You bet. The above ten statements (along with other statements) were used by your author in management surveys conducted in a cross-section of American companies. Included was a major chemical company, a large automobile manufacturer, a regional utility, an international service company, a leading food-products company, and a medium-sized agri-business. In all, 367 people participated in the surveys. Here are the composite results from the seven surveys:

SURVEY RESULTS

	SA %	A %	N %	D %	SD %
1. Well structured...	2	38	29	25	4
2. Understand goals..	2	32	17	38	10
3. Information tech...	2	32	26	33	6
4. Stimulated, chall...	34	46	9	7	1
5. Accountability...	4	31	24	36	4
6. Insights, actions...	5	39	23	27	5
7. Fear....	1	19	17	39	21
8. Know...expected...	27	56	7	8	1
9. Balance...	5	34	25	30	4
10. Well positioned...	11	49	24	13	2

Suppose the above were the responses from all the key people in a hypothetical emerging company called Alpha, Inc. What is the pulse of Alpha? Suppose further that Alpha's leading lights had an ambitious strategic plan for focusing the business on some sterling opportunities in the galaxy of possibilities surrounding the company. What is the likelihood of effective plan execution, given what you can see in the responses above. Think about it.

* * * * * * *

On a positive note, most of the respondents at Alpha found stimulation and challenge in their work (#4), and they generally knew what was expected of them (#8).

On the other hand, you will note that only about 40 percent of the respondents felt the structure–the organization design–was a positive force in Alpha's competitive posture. See statements #1 and #9. Organization design is usually a vital ingredient in the execution of a plan. The primary purpose of organization design should be to facilitate the execution of business strategy. More on this in Chapter 15.

Accountability (#5) and decision-making processes (#7) both received low favorable scores. If fear of making big mistakes interferes with decision-making at Alpha on a regular basis, it is probably a waste of time and energy for the business builders to preach innovation via risk taking or customer service via empowerment or focus via discipline. It is also quite possible that the feelings about fear and lack of accountability would never be uncovered by MBWA or its derivatives. Properly done, anonymous surveys can pick up such sentiments.

If the strategic planning at Alpha was aimed at producing important insights and actions, only a little more than four in ten key people were positive about the results according to statement #6. This showing suggests that there may be less than robust support for the execution of whatever plans have been made.

Communication, a perennial challenge in the best of times, may also need some attention at Alpha. In statement #2, nearly half of the respondents disagree that people at all levels have a clear understanding of Alpha's goals and objectives. Statement #3 may highlight another communication problem. A total of 39% do not feel the business unit management teams are making good use of information technology. Whether the teams are or not is somewhat academic; the feeling is that they are not. In large measure, feelings drive behavior.

Finally, the composite pulse of the organization is indicated in statement #10. It appears that six in ten key people feel Alpha is well positioned to be an effective competitor. Is this a healthy percentage? Good enough? Worrisome? If Alpha were your company, how would you feel about the response to #10? If Alpha were your company, what, if anything, would you do with the survey data?

The survey results suggest three propositions for the builders at hypothetical Alpha, Inc. to consider:

1. If they exist, the goals and objectives (as well as the rationale for them) do not seem to have penetrated very deeply into the organization. In addition, the strategic planning and decision-making processes may be inhibiting rather than enabling or ennobling. (Statements #2,#6,#7)

Commentary: Business management has a long tradition of hoarding information, as opposed to sharing it. Even in this infoweb age, in the rush of events many emerging companies operate primarily in a "need to know" mode reminiscent of wartime restrictiveness. Secrecy prevails. When a company's "most important assets" are unclear about the destination of the enterprise, many will take private roads to go somewhere of their own choosing.

2. Alpha's current structure is not particularly popular, and it may be serving as an anchor rather than a sail in terms of aiding competitiveness. (#1,#9)

Commentary: An organization design sets up relationships and suggest priorities. For example, is marketing senior to sales or vice versa? Or are these two functions equal? Is information sufficiently important to the enterprise for it to have a CIO (Chief Information

Officer) in the same way most businesses have a CFO (Chief Financial Officer)? The purpose of organization design is to induce desired behavior in the preparation and execution of plans. A problematic design can lead to weak plans and/or tepid execution.

3. A sizable percentage of the respondents ("key people") seem to know what is expected of them, are stimulated and challenged in their work, and yet do not feel accountable for the plans made, presumably the plans for building the enterprise. (#4,#8,#5)

Commentary: The lack of accountability may stem from one of several sources. Perhaps many respondents were not part of the planning process. As suggested in Chapter 10, it is best if the people who have to carry out plans are central to the preparation of those plans. The problem may stem from inconsistencies in the reward system of the enterprise. People will tilt toward doing what they get paid to do, and in the survey results they say they do know what is expected of them. If the rewards at Alpha pile up on the side of immediate performance with the materials at hand, executing plans aimed at focusing and longer-term competitiveness is likely to get short shrift.

Surveys are not high science. But, done properly, they can add some form and firmness to the messy job of taking the pulse of an enterprise. What does "done properly" include? Here are five guidelines:

1. Include statements (ask questions) only about subjects on which you honestly want input.

When you place a subject before a respondent, you immediately raise expectations. People will respond in hopes of contributing to the decisions and subsequent action. If expectations are dashed by silence or inactivity, cynicism will follow. You will be better off never having raised the issue.

2. Quickly feed composite survey results back to those who responded.

Bob Nelson, head of organization and development at the BBC in London put it this way: "...the cardinal rule of employee surveys is that the results, no matter how dire, must see the light of day, if for no other reason than employees will simply assume the worst if the results are not published."[18] The BBC surveys its people around the world approximately every 16 months.

3. Take action based on the survey results.

This, of course, is the proof of the pudding. Do you walk what you talk? When survey input–or any input–says something is amiss, do the leaders of the business respond appropriately? In the past decade, the business builders at GE have done a splendid job of tearing down bureaucracy and replacing it with just-do-it teamwork. Rather than surveys, the central method at GE has been what the people there call their Workout Program. In this program, groups of employees and managers meet to review everything from procedures to best practices. The whole idea is to stimulate opinions, openness, and ideas about the business. The central rule of conduct is quite simple: Managers must say yes or no to employee suggestions on the spot.[19] Note that it's O.K. to say no at GE. This is true in responding to survey results too. The issue is not that anything showing up negative in a survey must be fixed. The issue is that somebody listens and responds in a thoughtful manner.

4. Look for trends rather than absolutes.

It is more useful in practice to know that 50% of your people feel positive about the direction of the enterprise today compared to 30% a year ago than it is to worry about whether the 50% is good news or bad. People change. Their sentiments fluctuate day to day. Business life has a lot of variables. Repeated surveys provide a picture of how opinions are evolving over time.

5. Use survey results as agenda items to talk with people–individually and in groups.

Emerging companies change relatively quickly. The pace breeds uncertainties. Uncertainties accumulate and may undermine nimbleness, ingenuity, aggressiveness, and other happy features of the unfolding success story. One of the few antidotes to uncertainty is information. But many emerging company management teams are still in the dark ages when it comes to people-to-people communication skills. Innovation and technical black magic can often catapult a company into the air, but once it is airborne, it takes more and more people working together to maintain flight. Working together requires purposeful communication. Survey results can provide powerful ammunition for purposeful communication.

Strategic plans to focus a business must be executed well if there is to be a payoff. The sun is sinking on the notion that managers do the thinking and everyone else follows orders. They don't. Relentless progress beyond the survival stage requires informed, committed people working toward shared expectations. Builders of businesses miss a bet if they do not systematically take the pulse of their organizations to check on the vital signs. By picking important issues, obtaining input periodically, and following through, you can establish a feedback loop that will be a plus in constructing your enterprise for the long haul.

14
Managing
vs.
Doing

" The trick is to manage more and do less."
- Raymond O. Loen

From setting expectations to planning and taking the organizational pulse, the preceding chapters of this book suggest a heavy menu of activities for builders of businesses. Many of the recommended activities do not pay off immediately. Time spent on such matters—at the expense of activities that have an immediate impact—is often hard to justify. Builders in an emerging company must be able to prioritize focusing activities in the total scheme of things that consume their days.

Most people with leadership responsibilities got where they are by being good at doing something. They had (and have) certain technical or functional strengths important to the enterprise. These people frequently assimilated management responsibilities on the run. The central message of this chapter is that it is very important for business builders to distinguish clearly between managing work and the other kinds of work they do.

Managing is a distinct *kind* of work. It is different from non-managing work—not better, not more important, but different. Without a practical point of view about how managing differs from other work, it is unlikely that the ideas about focusing via strategic planning presented in this book—or ideas about any serious material on other managing subjects—will be applied. After finishing a book such as this, or a seminar, or a video, it is common for busy builders of companies to rub their hands together, nod their heads affirmatively, and then "get back to work" doing precisely what they were doing before the enriching educational experience! The fault does not lie entirely with the source of the material or the builder; the fault is evenly divided and reflects both a semantic problem and a lack of perspective on everyone's part.

Here is a very short story followed by an equally short exercise to illustrate the point about perspective.

> The Head Ski Company[20] is one of the all-time favorite business policy cases used in graduate classrooms across the country. Howard Head was an engineer/inventor who in 1950 founded a company to introduce metal skis to the world. By 1965, Head Ski was the U.S. market leader in the sale of high-priced metal skis. As President, Howard Head led his company through a number of ups and downs over its fifteen-year history, but in 1965 the company was well-positioned in a solid market, and it had plenty of cash as well as a high price/earnings (P/E) ratio on its publicly-traded stock. At that time, various expansion moves were being considered by the senior management team of the emerging Head Ski Company. The company could add fiberglass skis as well as boots and goggles to its product line, expand into retailing, or even diversify into clothing. Overall, there were a great number of opportunities—as well as new competitors—with which to deal.

The president's day was filled with a variety of activities. Decide which of them were managing activities, and which were actually non-managing activities? Check an answer to each question in one of the two columns.

EXERCISE

*Was Howard Head managing
when he ...*   Yes   No

1. Spent an afternoon with the president of a
   retail chain of stores, Head Ski's largest
   customer?   —   —

2. Solved a knotty design problem that had
   been perplexing his chief engineer for sev-
   eral weeks?   —   —

3. Visited the senior loan officer of the bank
   where the company did business to negoti-
   ate a loan?   —   —

4. Discussed with a European consultant a
   range of fabrics and colors for a new product line of Head Ski clothing that was un-
   der consideration?   —   —

5. Gave a speech to a noon gathering of stock
   analysts in New York City?   —   —

6. Took his regular walking tour through the
   plant in order to keep in touch with the
   people and processes?   —   —

7. Held a staff meeting with the officers of
   the Company to review cash-flow projections?   —   —

8. Interviewed several final job candidates for
   the position of controller, and made an of-
   fer to one of them?   —   —

9. Accompanied a recently promoted
   Vice-President of Sales to a national sporting goods convention in order to get the VP
   off to a good start with some of the
   industry's old timers?   —   —

10. Initiated an open discussion of corporate
    objectives at the regular Board of Direc-
    tors meeting?   —   —

Before taking a close look at the ten activities on the previous page, one by one, think about four issues that relate to the exercise:

A. What are the implications to the Head Ski Company if Howard Head, on taking the exercise, answers yes to all ten activities?

B. If Howard Head answers yes to all ten, how will most of the other key business builders in Head Ski probably answer similar questions in an exercise containing examples of their own day-to-day activities?

C. If all the senior people at Head Ski are busy with the kinds of activities shown, what activities are most likely *not* getting done?

D. What must happen at Head Ski Company if the enterprise is to keep on succeeding?

Starting from the bottom with issue D, most experienced hands would say that what the company needs if it is to continue to lead the parade in its industry is a well thought-out plan that provides for a continuing flow of new products and talent, a control/reporting system to keep track of the expanding empire, and so forth. *Rationally,* those needs are obvious to any practiced business builder. *Rationally,* they are probably obvious to Howard Head and his team. But in practice, according to the case, President Head spent most of his time on non-managing activities. Look back at the Exercise.

1. Was the president "managing" during the afternoon he spent with the company's largest customer? No, he was selling. *Selling isn't managing.*

2. Was the president managing as he worked out the solution to the design problem? No, he was doing engineering work. *Engineering isn't managing.*

3. Was Howard Head managing when he visited the bank to negotiate loan arrangements? No, he was doing the functional work of an individual. *Negotiating isn't managing.*

"Now wait a minute," you say, "all of these activities are part of Mr. Head's job. They have to be done. He *has* to do them! Who's kidding whom, here?" And you are partially right–the jobs do have to be done. Whether Mr. Head's time is best spent on them is a separate question. Here's where a point of view and perspective on managing vs doing enter the picture.

Every person who has management responsibilities in an emerging company is faced with a variety of tasks that typically consume all of his or her available time.

100% Of Available Time

Lacking an easy way to differentiate managing work from non-managing work, non-managing activities (selling, engineering, negotiating, etc.) will almost always usurp the managing work to be done for one or more of the following reasons:

• The manager has historically excelled in non-management activities. It was probably his or her technical performance as an individual that led to a promotion into a position with management responsibilities.

• Non-management activities are often spontaneous. They arise naturally, without being initiated or cultivated. The phone rings, the mail arrives, or a subordinate asks for assistance. ("Can you help me with this design problem?") Most often, there is a continuing flow of opportunities for a management person to contribute via his or her functional expertise.

- Non-management activities usually lead to concrete results. Orders are won or lost. A problem is solved. A loan is signed. Definite results can be very satisfying.

As a practical matter, *non-managing work is the work of an individual.* When Howard was selling, or engineering, or negotiating, he was "doing," that is, working to achieve a result by himself. And "doing" work with the momentum of personal history behind it and the high potential for immediate feedback has a proven capability to overshadow—push aside—managing work.

100% Of Available Time

In the words of management researcher and scholar, Louis A. Allen:

When called upon to perform management work and technical work during the same time period, a manager will tend to give first priority to technical work.[21]

What do we know about the people who need to mix these different kinds of work? Author Jon R. Katzenbach calls them Change Agents:

They're more flexible than ordinary general managers, and much more people oriented....They have a nice balance of capabilities: They are technically skilled people who are also very capable in personal relationships. They're an odd combination. On the one hand, they're tough decision-makers who are highly disciplined about performance results. But they also know how to get lots of people energized and aligned in the same direction.[22]

In short, managing is the task of achieving planned results through others. This doesn't mean *with* others, or *for* others, but *through* others in the same way that a basketball coach is responsible for the planned results of winning games. When he or she is coaching, he or she isn't dribbling the ball, guarding an opponent, or shooting a basket. To get the coaching job done, he or she must select and motivate people, set objectives, make plans, evaluate progress, and repeat the cycle.

Few builders of businesses, if any, can spend full time managing, i.e. coaching their teams. Most all are faced with the challenge of being player/coach. On occasion Howard Head *did* need to visit his company's largest customers and sell. No argument. But he wasn't managing when he did so! Moral: If all of an emerging company president's time is spent *doing,* the company's chance of continuing to succeed goes way down. What is needed is balance between time spent on managing and time spent doing the work of an individual. What is the proper mix?

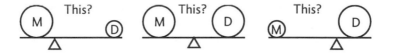

The right mix for any given person will vary with the nature of his or her responsibilities in the organization as well as with the size and complexity of the business. But the tendencies are clear. The larger and more complex the enterprise, the more critical it is for senior people to consciously spend increasing amounts of their time working to achieve planned results through others. On the next page the diagram, Need for Effective Managing, illustrates the idea.

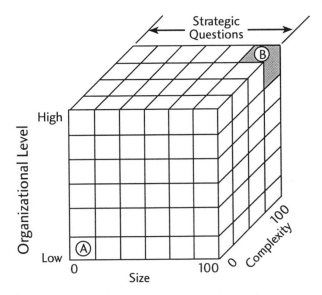

Need for Effective Managing

Emerging companies tend to gravitate from point A toward point B. Along the way, the managing practices of the builders of the business need to change if the enterprise is to continue succeeding. Head Ski Company was somewhere in the center of the cube. As head coach Bill Walsh puts it:

> *Whether you're a general, a CEO, or a football coach, finding a middle ground between the well-being of the people who work for you and the achievement of a goal is one of the trickiest aspects of leadership.*[23]

Does all this effort to differentiate managing from non-managing work have any payoff? It is your author's experience that people without perspective on the issue have trouble focusing their businesses. They are reluctant to spend time on the subjects in this book or on developing people, organizational design, and other "soft-side," managing/leadership matters.

Returning to the Exercise, in questions 1, 2, and 3 Howard Head was doing the work of an individual contributor. He was not achieving results through others. The issue is not whether or not he should visit a customer, solve an engineering problem, or negotiate a loan. Perhaps he should. And the same goes for activities 4 and 5—selecting fabrics and colors and giving speeches. The issue is that while the president may feel compelled to do these things, he's not managing when he does them. And if all the key people in the company follow his lead, the emerging Head Ski company is going to be bypassed by the company's more astute competitors.

Activities 6 and 7 in the Exercise are in a gray zone. Certainly keeping in touch with people through tours and meetings may be managing as defined here. It depends on the leader's mind set. Did the president tour and observe in an effort to help various people grow and develop? Or was he merely showing the colors to let everyone know that the ace problem-solver and source of wisdom was still around and available?

Activities 8, 9, and 10 have to do with achieving results through others, and they are representative of the kinds of activities to which the key people in emerging companies must willingly shift a good part of their time and energy. Great companies have been built by single individuals in the past, and there will be some great ones built essentially by individuals in the future. But the more common model for the days ahead will be great companies constructed by teams of business builders working together in a purposeful, focused effort.

Earlier (page 148), four issues were raised about the Exercise. Issues A and B revolved around the implications to the Head Ski Company if all of its senior people answered yes to most of the questions on the list. If everyone is busy doing, managing will not get done. In an emerging company the job of managing *must* get done or the company will get out of focus and peak out at a point equal to the sum of various individual efforts. The enterprise may well cease to emerge; it might even begin to recede.

Issues C and D involve, in essence, a definition of managing work. The subject is an evolving one, and it has been analyzed in various ways. Sixty years ago, in the 1930s, you knew about general managing in a progressive company if you understood several basic functions such as industrial engineering, accounting, and sales. That was the start of what was then termed *scientific management*. In the 1940s, some knowledge of human relations was added to the mix. Various scientific experiments unexpectedly uncovered the fact that the output of employees was not merely a physical given. There were psychological aspects to running companies. People could be motivated! Managing became a broader subject.

In the 1950s and 1960s, other functional specialties were added to the list of things a general manager needed to know, or at least understand. First, marketing came to be seen as more than just the sum of advertising, selling, and pricing. Marketing was followed by breakthroughs in techniques of financial analysis and reporting, and a busy business builder had additional functional knowledge to absorb. But something happened during this period that was even more important than these breakthroughs. The idea of managing as a distinct body of knowledge worthy of study (like law or medicine) gathered momentum. The rapid expansion of the economy in the 1960s, along with the growth in size of domestic institutions such as corporations, universities, and governments, generated a large demand for more "managers." Managing by objectives (See Chapter 2) was introduced and commercialized by a number of consultants. Alfred P. Sloan, Jr.'s, *My Years With General Motors*, became an instant best seller when it was published in 1963. The book greatly boosted managing as a discipline and as a profession. The book has since become a classic; the cover of the most recent edition features praise for the contents by Bill Gates of Microsoft.

Meanwhile, in the schools of business around the country, certain faculty members were drawing together the threads of thought about managing that ran back in time to earlier thinkers on the subject, from the classical (management process) school associated with Henri Fayol (1841-1925), through the behavioral or human-relations school given visibility by Elton Mayo (1880-1949), to the quantitative school of more recent vintage. Managing was, indeed, a distinct and expanding kind of work.

The result? Today, the idea of managing as a discrete field worthy of research and study is well established. There are many ways to segment the field, but one practical way for busy people in emerging companies to look at it is this:

The builders of an emerging company need to...
  1. Understand the **Operating Environment**
       (Internal & External)
  2. Set **Expectations**
  3. Decide on **Strategy**
  4. Adapt the **Organization Design**
  5. Adapt the **Organization Processes**
  6. Adjust their **Style**–Managing & Leading
  7. Get better at working with **People**
  8. Cultivate a desired **Culture**

This list of eight key managing variables is meant to be reasonably comprehensive and practical, though not exhaustive. Suffice it to say that a person or a team proficient in the subjects will most likely do well in achieving planned results through others. Most of this book has been directed at the first three subjects which make up the leading edge of focusing your business: Operating environment, expectations, and strategy. A complete plan for a business, however, should reflect due consideration of all eight subjects plus the financial implications of the building program.

In summary, senior people in companies on the move in competitive industries need perspective on what is and what is not managing work. An ability to distinguish the two and to put the distinction into practice is important—probably even critical. Smart managing can be a significant part of a company's competitive edge. Intel and Microsoft come to mind as examples of companies that emerged in the 1990s in large part *because* of effective managing. A results-through-others orientation leads to dynamic plans that have plan implementation built in from the start. Focusing a business is a continuing process of identifying and moving into new territory while gracefully giving up some of the old. This process must be *managed* as the capabilities of an enterprise are transformed over time.

15
Building for the Long Haul

"...and the secret to survival is knowing what to throw away and knowing what to keep."
- from the song, *The Gambler*, by Kenny Rogers

There is a typical cycle for management buzzwords. It goes something like this. A new term is conceived, proclaimed orally and in writing, and then picked up by consultants, academics, and a few astute management teams. Then the term is generalized beyond its original application, overused, and–finally–just plain misused to the point where it passes, muddled, into the etymological swamp in which many companies fish. Eileen Shapiro in her book, *Fad Surfing in the Boardroom*, defines the cycle as "the practice of riding the crest of the latest management panacea and then paddling out again just in time to ride the next one." She goes on to say, "...always absorbing for managers and lucrative for consultants...it is frequently disastrous for organizations."[24]

Focusing can be a fad. Likewise, strategic planning. It takes determined effort on the part of those who build a business to make sure these practices have sturdy roots in the enterprise. A company that is successful in emerging against larger, entrenched, multifaceted giants *and* against smaller, more specialized competitors will need all the focus it can muster. A company that is focused is one in which all the members of the organization are a flock of migrating birds winging a twisting course across the sky in a synchronous, almost effortless motion as they response in unison to plans, fresh opportunities, and unwanted surprises.

What is the recipe to achieve such a state? Many of the ingredients have been suggested earlier in this book: a common vocabulary, clear expectations, staying in touch with the organization, a planning process that produces decisions and commitments, perspective on the work of managing. These ingredients can be stirred together in different ways, according to taste. The consultants at McKinsey & Company, Inc. developed one view of the sequence of steps involved in moving from a "Meet the budget" orientation to a "Create the Future" orientation. Their thinking is illustrated in the diagram, Phases in Evolution of Strategic Decision Making.[25]

The Value System shown across the bottom of the diagram describes the mind set of the leadership. Note the four Phases, from Financial Planning to Strategic Management, and how parallel they are in many respects to the Hierarchy of Planning Techniques covered in Chapters 7-9. The point of this diagram is that building for the long haul is neither mystical nor rocket science. Doing so requires the systematic use of all the basic tools in the managing tool box to reconfigure an enterprise as time passes. The eight basic tools (as outlined in Chapter 14) are...

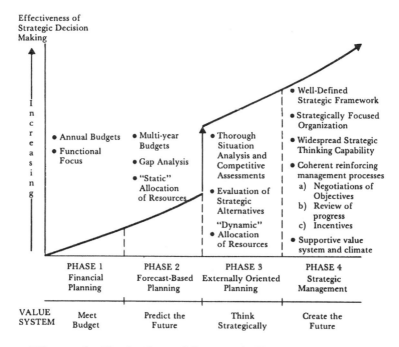

Phases in Evolution of Strategic Decision Making

> Understand the **Operating Environment**
>   (Internal & External)
> Set **Expectations**
> Decide on **Strategy**
> Adapt the **Organization Design**
> Adapt the **Organization Processes**
> Adjust their **Style**–Managing & Leading
> Get better at working with **People**
> Cultivate a desired **Culture**

Now, rather than dealing any further with *pre*scription, consider a *de*scription of how an emerging company might operate if it has–by whatever means–arrived at that state of existence labeled "focused." Here are six characteristics the careful observer of such an enterprise might discern:

1. A widespread respect for and sensitivity to the operating environment–starting with the needs of present and potential customers.
2. A well-understood and accepted calendar of events that guarantees the primary builders of the business a "window" on the key issues and operations of the company.
3. A responsive openness in key people that reflects a sense of shared purpose, identification with the company, and confidence in their professional future.
4. A performance evaluation and reward system that is relatively subtle and oriented to the longer term, and that focuses attention on a few results while allowing wide latitude in day-to-day operations.
5. A well orchestrated, albeit lean, "farm system" for developing both the managing and doing talent vital to the future of the enterprise.
6. An entrepreneurial, can-do attitude that acknowledges the temporary nature of today's products or services and market definitions.

A detailed consideration of these six characteristics follows.

1. A widespread respect for and sensitivity to the environment–starting with the needs of present and potential customers. It's not unusual for eighty to ninety percent of the people in an emerging company to give virtually zero attention to those who are paying the bills. Even in many service businesses, which should presumably know better, customers are often abstractions rather than people. Yet being tightly tuned to the stark reality of the total operating environment is the mark of companies that seem to land on their feet regardless of changes in the economy, competitive moves, and social/political turbulence. Such tuning is not bred with a few wall posters exalting the customer. Personal contact is the most efficient single method for schmoozing with reality. The controller, line foreman, or technician who visits a complaining customer's facility for a first-hand exposure to the wrath returns a wiser team member. The emerging company whose officers each spend a minimum of a day a month in the field is going to make more informed decisions today on the issues that produce tomorrow.

Commandment Two in your author's *Ten Commandments for Building a Growth Company* reads:

Define the business of the enterprise in terms of what is to be bought, precisely by whom, and why. *Businesses are organs of society that perform tasks associated with providing most goods and services the public decides it wishes to own and use. Under this capitalistic system, a business can prosper to the extent it performs its particular tasks effectively and efficiently within the law. The nature of the tasks to be performed usually changes over time as those served change. The successful company predicts and responds to its chosen customers' needs.* Customers, therefore, define the business. *At all times, some customers are growing in their ability to buy; others are declining. The astute manager ascertains which is which.*[26]

How many of your key people who are not involved in sales spend a significant part of their time in the field?

2. A well-understood and accepted calendar of events that guarantees the primary builders of the business a "window" on the key issues and operations of the company. As suggested in several places earlier, one of the prices of success paid by an emerging company is that the people with the best noses for the action get promoted to positions farther and farther from the action as the company prospers. The ace salesperson is elevated to district manager; the sharpest engineer rises to department head; the strongest person in the lab becomes a vice president. This may not be a formula for the long-term success of the enterprise! The only proven antidote is a process that systematically forces important issues and operational problems to the surface for all to see. The fundamentals of such processes have been described in this book: planning units, sorting techniques, the primacy of line management, etc.

Do the leaders of your enterprise have something approaching a fingertip familiarity with each of the major components of your enterprise?

3. A responsive openness in key people that reflects a sense of shared purpose, identification with the company, and confidence in their professional future. This may sound a little old-fashioned, but get inside a company on the move and you will find these characteristics. Companies built on an entrepreneurial base often succeed because they have "driven" women and men–people at work on a common destiny. Otherwise the long hours, nervous energy, tenacious determination, and explosive creativeness just wouldn't happen. Extending the excitement of the early days is one of the great challenges in building for the long haul. Few management teams do it well. Every large company of today was once entrepreneurial, but most of them have been unable to hang onto the spirit in a meaningful way.

A responsive openness is something that originates inside people. Psychologists say that it can occur only in an atmosphere from which fear is absent. Fear of what? Fear of mistakes, censure, or even failure in an organizational sense. If an atmosphere exists in which there is a low tolerance for fresh ideas, dissent, or contrary opinions, then only the surface deposits of available human resources are going to be mined. Each boss is the reference point for those around. He or she establishes and reinforces the primary working condition, for better or worse. Collectively, the business builders in an emerging company make it easy—or hard—to share in a purpose, to identify with the organization.

Now all the evidence of psychiatry . . . shows that membership in a group sustains a man, enables him to maintain his equilibrium under the ordinary shocks of life, and helps him to bring up children who will in turn be happy and resilient. If his group is shattered around him, if he leaves a group in which he was a valued member, and if, above all, he finds no new group to which he can relate himself, he will under stress, develop disorders of thought, feeling, and behavior . . . The cycle is vicious; loss of group membership in one generation may make men less capable of group membership in the next. The civilization that, by its very process of growth, shatters small group life will leave men and women lonely and unhappy.

— George C. Homans, *The Human Group*[27]

To what extent have you and your key people progressed beyond e-mail, bulletin board notices, and an annual party or picnic toward regular, conscious acts aimed at cultivating a mini-society obsessed with building for the long haul?

4. A performance evaluation and reward system that is relatively subtle and oriented to the longer term, and that focuses attention on a few results while allowing wide latitude in day-to-day operations. It is common knowledge today that strategic plans superimposed on compensation systems based on immediate performance criteria are plans that will probably be under-executed. Not only do grand plans get tepid attention, trust and teamwork are eroded by the obvious slips between cup and lip. This problem can be particularly acute in rapidly growing companies where it is relatively easy to delay longer-term investments in people, information systems, cost controls, quality, and other matters that don't cry out for immediate attention. As Thomas A. Stewart puts it in a *Fortune* article:

> *You can blather on endlessly about teamwork and trust, but if your people don't see what's in it for them, don't expect them to listen.*[19]

Are your key people asked for long-range plans and thinking but paid for this year's ROI?

5. A well orchestrated, albeit lean, "farm system" for developing both the managing and doing talent vital to the future of the enterprise. Take a look at some of your favorite leading companies, the ones with track records stretching back over a decade or more. Chances are good that most of them have evolved extensive internal programs for identifying, developing, and boosting their outstanding performers over time. Chances are even better that there are multiple, qualified, *trained* replacements for key openings in these companies as they grow. There are people with the necessary strategic skills and personal characteristics to take on assignments to build, hold, or harvest different parts of the enterprise as planned. And there always seems to be a small number of truly exceptional people who can be pulled up and plugged into unusual opportunities with high-risk/ high-payoff potential.

How do the builders keep costs down while running a personnel farm system with substance? The president of an emerging, international company based in Switzerland never visits any one of his company's twelve subsidiaries without taking along a junior. The CEO of an upstart Los Angeles service company requires that each of her dozen key people spend at least one day a month out of the office making contacts outside of his or her functional specialty. Each of six senior researchers in a fast growing Palo Alto chemical company are required to devote a minimum of six days a year to on-site customer visits at which no *existing* company business is discussed. These are examples of simple actions senior builders can instigate to develop their human resource base without incurring the expense of a formal training effort of some kind.

At some point in time, a focused company will probably reach a size where the simple, informal efforts of key people need to be institutionalized to some extent. Then internal management development programs, manpower planning, career pathing, and individualized incentive systems all become candidates for organized attention and investment. The important danger to avoid is a smorgasbord approach in which too much human-resource enthusiasm leads to too many programs in too many flavors, with indigestion the end result! The personnel farm system should support the strategic plan of the enterprise and be held strictly accountable for measurable results. If a reasonably direct linkage between the system and the plan cannot be readily identified and articulated, the farm system probably needs an overhaul (or harvesting!).

6. An entrepreneurial, can-do attitude that acknowledges the temporary nature of today's products or services and market definitions. It is appropriate to close this chapter on building for the long haul and the book itself on the high ground of entrepreneurship. This is a term enjoying a resurgence of respectability and popularity with the advent of computers on a chip, biomagic, software, Internet devices, and many other manifestations of a society ripe with opportunity. For a long time entrepreneurs were only slightly more socially acceptable than outlaws. Now entrepreneurship is front-page material around the world.

How do alert business builders perpetuate entrepreneurship? Organization design can help. Dividing and redividing the whole into discrete, manageable pieces can keep important, operating decisions close to the customer interface. Organization processes can help. They are meant to work horizontally across an enterprise to bring together the best and the brightest in the service of building the business. Strategic planning can help. The practical alternative to trying to be all things to all people is to be some things to some people. This is focusing. Choices have to be made, and the act and fact of making such choices is in itself renewing, entrepreneurial.

Planning and executing plans is not the whole story of what builders of businesses do—particularly in emerging companies that are still in a highly formative state. True builders must be alert to opportunities, the kinds of opportunities that cannot be planned. Who can anticipate an unexpected joint venture offer, a research breakthrough, a surprise in the level of government spending, or a competitor stumbling? What comprehensive planning *can* do, however, is to clarify expectations; crystallize the current reality—internal and external; identify excess baggage; and generally aim the enterprise at a chosen intersection of opportunity and capability.

Steve Brandt

REFERENCES

1. Adapted from article by Larry E. Greiner, "Evolution and Revolution as Organizations Grow," *Harvard Business Review*, July-August 1972, p. 41.
2. Fred R. Bleakley, "Many Firms See Gains of Cost-Cutting Over, Push to Lift Revenues," *Wall Street Journal*, July 5, 1996, p.1.
3. James Aley, "The Theory That Made Microsoft," *Fortune*, April 29, 1996, p. 65.
4. David P. Baron, "Integrated Strategy," *California Management Review*, Vol. 37, No. 2, Winter 1995.
5. "Destroying the Old Hierarchies," *Forbes*, June 3, 1996, p. 62.
6. Robert N. Noyce, "Creativity by the Numbers," *Harvard Business Review*, May-June 1980.
7. Peter Drucker, "The Network Society," *Wall Street Journal*, March 29, 1995, editorial page.
8. Michael Treacy & Fred Wiersema, *The Discipline of Market Leaders*, (Reading, MA: Addison Wesley, 1995), p. 47.
9. "Sun Microsystems," *Business Week*, January 22, 1996, pp. 68-70.
10. Steven C. Brandt, *Entrepreneuring: The Ten Commandments for Building a Growth Company, 2nd Edition* (Friday Harbor, WA: Archipelago Publishing, 1996), p. 92.
11. Samuel. A. Culbert, Mind-Set Management (New York: Oxford University Press: 1996), p. 3.
12. Bill Walsh, "When Past Perfect Isn't," *Forbes ASAP*, June 3, 1996, p. 18.

13. Tom Abate, "Mulling Work, Business in the New Millennium," *San Francisco Examiner*, September 10, 1995, p. B-1.
14. "How a Tough Boss Managed to Salvage a Messy Unit at GM," *Wall Street Journal*, June 3, 1996, p. 1.
15. Jon R. Katzenbach & Douglas K. Smith, "The Discipline of Teams," *Harvard Business Review*, March-April 1993, Reprint # 93207.
16. Steven C. Brandt, "Are You Walkin' What You're Talkin'," *Stanford Business School Magazine*, June 1990, p. 16.
17. Kenneth Blanchard & Spencer Johnson, *One Minute Manager* (New York: Berkely Books, 1983), p. 67. Copyright 1982 by Blanchard Family.
18. Erik Ipsen, "Employee Surveys Put Boorish Bosses on Notice," *International Herald Tribune*, April 24, 1996, p. 1.
19. Thomas A. Stewart, "Why Value Statements Don't Work," *Fortune,* June 10, 1996, p. 137-8.
20. "Head Ski Company, Inc.," a Harvard Business School case study distributed by the Intercollegiate Case Clearing House, Boston, MA.
21. Louis A. Allen. *Professional Management: New Concepts and Proven Practices* (New York: McGraw-Hill, 1973), p. 60.
22. Stratford Sherman, "Wanted: Company Change Agents," *Fortune*, December 11, 1995, p. 197.
23. Bill Walsh, "What Price Glory," *Forbes ASAP*, February 26, 1996, p.16.
24. Stanley W. Angrist, "Cutting Through the Jargon," *Wall Street Journal*, June 4, 1996, p. A12. This is a review of Eileen Shapiro, *Fad Surfing in the Boardroom* (Boston: Addison-Wesley, 1996).

25. Frederick W. Gluck, Stephen P. Kaufman and A. Steven Walleck, "The Evolution of Strategic Management," *McKinsey Staff Paper*, October, 1978, p. 4.
26. Steven C. Brandt, *Entrepreneuring: The Ten Commandments for Building a Growth Company, 2nd Edition* (Friday Harbor, WA: Archipelago Publishing, 1996), p. 32.
27. William G. Ouchi & Alfred M. Jaeger, "Type Z Organization: A Corporate Alternative to Village Life," *Stanford Business School Alumni Bulletin*, Fall 1977-78, p. 13.

Readings

Reading I

Creativity by the Numbers

An interview with Robert N. Noyce

"Intel measures absolutely everything and innovation flourishes."

In an inflationary era, the tiny computer on a chip that Intel makes is a dream product—as it becomes more efficient and more powerful, it becomes cheaper. With the cost falling by 30% a year, applications for microcomputers have cropped up everywhere, and the limits to their usefulness are nowhere in sight. Because of their small size and reliability, they have not only enhanced all the major functions of the computer but they have invaded the consumer market in digital watches and electronic games, to name only a few of their myriad uses.

It was at Intel Corporation, of Santa Clara, in the heart of California's "Silicon Valley," that the microprocessor, the specialized semiconductor chip that contains the "brain" of a computer, was invented in 1971. While maintaining its lead in the technology of microprocessors, Intel has developed more than twenty highly innovative products that have made the company an acknowl-

Reprinted by permission of the *Harvard Business Review*, "Creativity by the Numbers," interview with Robert N. Noyce (May-June 1980). Copyright © 1980 by the President and Fellows of Harvard College; all rights reserved.

edged leader in the semiconductor industry. By putting as much as 10% of all revenue into R&D every year, Intel has managed consistently to keep ahead of the competition with new products, and, as others have tried to catch up, it has enjoyed profit margins over 20%, twice those of the rest of the industry.

Intel's revenues increased each year from 1976 to 1978 by 43% compounded. In the next couple of years, it expects to reach $1 billion in sales.

Robert N. Noyce is vice-chairman of Intel. He attended Grinnell College where he was elected to Phi Beta Kappa, and Massachusetts Institute of Technology, from which he received his Ph.D. in physics. He was on the research staff of the Shockley Semiconductor Laboratory, where he was involved in the design and development of silicon transistors. In 1959, with eight defectors from the Shockley Laboratory, he started a semiconductor division for Fairchild Camera and Instrument. While at Fairchild, as director of research, he helped develop the integrated circuit which was the precursor and prerequisite to the microprocessor. With Gordon Moore, another scientist-executive, Noyce left Fairchild in 1968 to start Intel. They were joined within a year by Andrew Grove, who had been associate director of research at Fairchild. Moore is now chairman and chief executive officer of Intel, and Grove is president and chief operating officer. President Carter presented the National Medal of Science to Noyce in January of this year for his work on semiconductor devices, especially on integrated circuits.

In this interview, conducted and edited by Lynn M. Salerno, assistant editor, HBR wanted to find out from Robert Noyce what it is like always to be the front runner in a fast-moving industry (it is "working on the edge of disaster"); his views on management of scientists ("they love to be measured"); and whether Intel experiments with flexible workweeks ("very hesitatingly"); about Intel's highly successful strategy ("we build on strength and try to stay out of competition where we're weak"). Finally, in a setting where even the president often wears a gold chain instead of a tie, Noyce described the environment as "confident, but not relaxed."

HBR: From its beginning, Intel has had a spectacular record. What's the secret of your success? Did you have a specific management philosophy from the start?

Robert N. Noyce: No, you didn't have to then. In a small organization there's enough communication so that the objectives are very clearly defined to begin with. If you can't communicate with only 25 people, your communication skills are pretty awful. So our organization was very sharply focused. We knew what product we were going after; everybody understood that very well. That was almost enough of a statement of objectives to last through the first couple of years.

What is the management role now?

Now we've run out of the collective experience of everyone. There's only one member of the board who has ever worked for a company larger than Intel— as Intel is today. And consequently, we feel that we're plowing new ground in terms of how we organize, how we do things, how we keep focus.

How do you keep focus?

Well, the thing that we've been concentrating on recently is the culture. What makes Intel Intel? A lot of it is what has evolved because of the personalities of the people around. It is MBO practiced all the way through. I think there's a lot of lip service given to MBO, and it's not practiced. But here everybody writes down what they are going to do and reviews how they did it, how they did against those objectives, not to management, but to a peer group and management. So that's also a communication mechanism between various groups, various divisions, etc.

Do you have a formal way to do that, then?

Yes, and it's pretty well built into the system. There is an openness, a willingness to discuss problems, identify them, which is not confrontational but rather, "Hey, I've got a problem. Here's how it's going." The executive staff, which basically consists of all the division managers, is truly an executive staff. They worry about the whole business, not just their own business, although they have the primary responsibility for their own business. There is very little in the way of staffers, as such. Staff work is done by line management as a secondary assignment. If we have a recruiting problem or a special project that needs to be done, we take a division general manager and say, "Okay, that's your secondary assignment for now."

How long have you had this kind of arrangement?

We just never have built a staff. We've always used line management for that kind of a function. I think that the way the business planning is done may be unique in terms of breaking the business into what we call strategic business segments. A committee is formed of the people, usually middle managers and below and a few senior managers, who make strategies, operate, identify trends, and identify the resources needed for operating that business segment. So that's a great training ground for oncoming management.

You don't have a separate planning function, then?

No, strategic planning is imbedded in the organization. It is one of the primary functions of line managers. They buy into the program; they carry it out. They're determining their own future, so I think the motivation for doing it well is high. Now that is not to say that we won't call on other resources. If we have a product area that we don't know much about, we certainly will call in a market research organization or whatever to give us more information to work on. But it is not a planning function that reports to the president, and it has no interaction with the organization.

Are there other important features of the culture?

The other essential aspect of the culture is that we expect people to work hard. We expect them to be here when they are committed to be here; we measure absolutely everything that we can in terms of performance.

Don't you find that approach difficult with the management of scientists?

I don't think it's difficult at all, because they're used to it. You know the old story about the scientist is that if you can't put a number to it, you don't know what the hell you're talking about. Well, as an example, customer service is poor—how poor? Let's measure what the response time is when a letter comes in, and we'll plot that versus time. Let's measure how many of the commitments on delivery schedules are met, how many are met in a week, how many are more than a month late.

What kind of people do you look for to work at Intel?

I think that the people we want to attract are, in general, high achievers. High achievers love to be measured, when you really come down to it, because otherwise they can't prove to themselves that they're achieving.

Or that anybody cares whether they are or not?

Yes, the fact that you are measuring them says that you do care. Then they're willing to work—they're not only willing but eager to work in that kind of environment. We've had people come in who have never had an honest review of their work. We get senior managers who come in, and we say, "Okay, in your six-month review, or your annual review, here are the things that you did poorly, here are the things you did well." A lot of these people have never heard that they ever did anything poorly. It's the new culture of our schools, you know, no grades. Everybody passes. We just don't happen to believe in that. We believe that people do want to be praised. So we try to do that.

That's an interesting outlook.

Even schools are beginning to move back to giving grades again. It was an aberration, I think, that occurred during the Vietnam War that was a very poor trend in our educational environment and was very poor training for people who wanted to go out into competitive society.

How do you keep making this a challenging place to work?

I think it's because people have the control of their own destiny, and they get measured on it. They get their M&M candies for every job, as one of our business instructors always said. It's now getting to be a real challenge because the billion-dollar company is clearly in view in the next year or so. The question is whether we can do it right. A great deal of effort goes into thinking about how we plan it, how we operate it, and how we build incentives into it. Where are we going? Are we going where we want to go? How do we win at this game called business? And, as I say, I think that our team is made of high achievers who really want to do that. They still see plenty of challenges.

Is there a lot of internal competition?

Well, there isn't the political infighting that you often see in companies. The direction is very carefully and definitely set, and everybody understands that. It's partly because of the way it's set—for both the MBO system and the strategic planning system. There just isn't any room for politics in the organization. It is very quickly rooted out. Someone who's crawling over someone else's body just doesn't get very far.

How does it get weeded out, though? The culture's strong enough?

No, I think the information is open enough so that what the individual manager is doing is put under a microscope once every six months by all his peers. His peers know all those games, too, so politics just doesn't work. He doesn't get any support from his peers if he's doing that. It's an interactive company. Most of the divisions are heavily dependent on another organization that will let them get their job done.

You tried a three-day workweek some time back and that didn't work out. What is the situation today?

We still have a three-day week in Portland. If you have a capital-intensive activity, how many hours a week can you use it? What we do is run four 12-hour shifts on three days; so, 36 times 4 equals 144 hours a week, instead of three 40-hours, or 120 hours per week use of the equipment. It is simply a question of efficient use of the capital equipment.

So it wasn't a plan for trying a flexible workweek. Do you experiment with that kind of thing at all here?

Very hesitatingly. There are too many other parts of our society that are geared around the five-day week. The kids are in school five days a week. How does mama arrange to go to work? What happens to the family life if you take those work patterns and make them different from the rest of the family? In general, it doesn't work very well. It's sort of like a graveyard shift; there's a different group of people than on the day shift.

There seems to be a lot of control here. Is that a correct impression?

Oh, it's a very disciplined organization. Very disciplined. And we pride ourselves on our discipline. Did you see the little graph as you came in the door there, the Late List? It gives the percentage of people who come in after 8:10.

Doesn't that bother the people working here?

Yes, it bothers a lot of people. But they get used to it. And it becomes a point of pride after a while. It's another way of saying to people that they're valuable to us. How can we do our work if they're not here? Intel is the only place I've ever worked where an 8:00 a.m. meeting starts at 8:00 a.m.

Do you have any way for employees to get their gripes up the pipeline?

Well, initially, when the company was smaller, Gordon [Moore, Intel chairman] and I would have lunch every Thursday with a random group of employees. Now, that has broken down. You can't be very effective when you have 10,000 employees in the United States alone. Our total employment is over 15,000. But the lunch discussions are held at smaller group levels, and you'll find that if you walk around here at noon nearly every conference room has some sort of a lunch going on in it.

Are the employees expected to come?

No. Originally, my secretary would take an employee list and just invite the first 10 names and then the next 10 names, so it was alphabetical. Sometimes if we had a particular thing we wanted to probe, we'd take an interest group— people with common interests, all the personnel people, all of the college kids who had come in six months ago, or something like that—to get a different view on it. But usually it was a random selection. So if they were busy that day, they'd be invited next week, and so forth, down the list. We used to get through all employees in those days. They were invited at least twice a year. It did, I think, give you a sensitivity to what people were thinking out there. We heard a lot of bitches, and we got a lot of suggestions. We still do.

You have a rather Spartan office. Is it typical of executive offices here?

Yes, I'd say so, for the older ones. The newer ones? There are none.

What do you have instead of offices?

The typical office landscaping sort of thing; no solid walls, open plan. Modular units that you can shift around as needed. In all the new buildings there are loads of conference rooms, so if you have to chew something you go in the conference rooms.

What if you have a private telephone call? Should you wait until lunchtime?

What kind of a private phone call would you have? I think that's part of the open communication. There are no secrets. I know the first time I started to think about it, it was shocking, but I had no hesitation to sit in any of those open offices and call nearly anyone. Occasionally I will use a conference room in one of the other buildings to make a phone call, but there really are just very few things when you stop to think about it that need to be handled that way. It's a habit to think that your phone calls are all confidential. But they aren't. Most people aren't interested. If the guy that's sitting next to you is somebody you trust and he overhears what you're saying, it doesn't matter very often.

Do most people like the open arrangement?

Yes, and there's a reason for it. We're social characters. Being locked in a box all day is not a very happy kind of situation when you get right down to it. Also, we try studiously to avoid the appurtenances of power. When we redo an office area we upgrade it a little bit. Part of it is an antisnob kind of a feeling.

Is there any kind of dress code?

You'll notice walking around here that less than 10% of the executives have a tie on. In fact, a lot of males here wear gold chains instead.

Was dress ever important here?

Yes. Ten years ago certainly I wouldn't have thought of coming into the office without a tie except on Saturday or Sunday or off hours, or something like that. It's much looser now. And if I'm not visiting somebody from outside the company, I will probably not wear a tie, probably not even wear a jacket. I will put on a sport shirt. It's sometimes shocking to people who come from the East Coast, although they're getting acclimated to it. They meet the president, and he's wearing a sport shirt and a gold chain.

Would you call this a relaxed atmosphere?

I don't think you could call it relaxed. A confident environment, but not a relaxed one. One of the problems we have when people come in from other companies is that they just don't believe the intensity of Intel. They're not used to it. We're in an intensely competitive industry where change is very rapid, and there is no resting on your laurels because you'll get wiped out next year if you just sit back.

Doesn't that take an awful toll on people?

It does on some.

Do you have a company psychiatrist?

No, but we have lost some people. In particular, during both the recessions in 1971 and 1975, a lot of people left the industry and just never came back, feeling that it was not a relaxed place. But then we go back to the high achievers, the people who want to be where the action is. The crew is very young. The average age of the population around here is far younger than in the old established businesses, partially because Intel is only 12 years old. But also it's because we are very actively recruiting straight out of school.

When you started your bubble memory capacity, Intel Magnetics, you got three people who came from Hewlett-Packard to start it. Why did you do that instead of starting the project with people here?

It's a different technology. We had no particular expertise in it. We felt that the entrepreneurial start-up in a new field like that was the best way to get ivory tower types to focus on the real problem. That's an unfair characterization of those guys because they're certainly interested in the commercialization of bubble memories, but it was a separable entity that you could do on an entrepreneurial basis. I think it's been effective.

You think that's a good way to expand your capabilities?

Oh, yes. It's a question whether it's related to your current activities. When it's not an evolution of your current activities, I think it's extremely dangerous do it that way. We try to keep the incentives, in terms of options and so forth, pretty consistent with the outside start-up and with people who are already here, so that it's equitable. And if the outsiders are enormously successful, they'll do better than the people here; if they are not as successful, people who are already here will do better, so it's a good incentive.

Do you try to find future markets by making the product yourself, or do you have people here who just study it without making it?

I'd say that in terms of the market areas that we're carving out, they're sort of the natural extension of the technology that we're doing. The only significant acquisition we've ever made was a Texas company, MRI, which is a software company. We did buy a watch company when digital watches were first coming along, but it was, in a sense, an entrepreneurial situation. It had 13 employees in it.

That didn't really work out?

It didn't work for us. We thought it was a technology game, and it turned out to be a merchandising game. That's just not our game. What we're doing is what we see as the logical next step of what we have to do. For instance, in selling the microcomputer chips, we had to provide instrumentation to let the designer design with those chips because it wasn't available somewhere else. But that was an essential part of getting the microcomputer established in the market. If we are going to do a good job of designing microcomputers, we have to know more about software. So the software company was a major acquisition in terms of buying a capability that we didn't have, but that we saw as a necessary layer of capability on top of the ones we already had.

Are some companies dipping into your field so they can find out more about your business?

Sure, Hewlett-Packard is getting significantly into the semiconductor business. Burroughs is, and so on. And it's important that they know more about this business because it's an essential tool for them. It's also important that we know more about their business because it's an essential market for us.

Are the lines starting to blur, moving up and also moving down?

Yes. Making semiconductors is becoming an essential technology to the computer industry, so they are participating in it. The computer is, you know, essentially where the semiconductor industry is going, so we're moving into some fringes of their business. The technology is driving us there, simply because if you're going to make ever more complex things, you are going to be making computers. That's the major complex thing that is being built with the semiconductor. It might turn out to be a calculator or a controller for the tape recorder or the engine controller for an automobile, but it's still a computer in one sense or another.

What's going to be the end of all this?

Oh, I don't know. I think it's that people do well what they do well, and they succeed at what they do well.

There's not going to be a lot of bumping of heads?

There hasn't been particularly, no. The high-volume products are purchased in the so-called merchant market for semiconductors. The highly specialized ones, for which there is very little volume, have been made by computer companies for themselves because we wouldn't. We have no interest in making them. Computer companies are not interested in manufacturing the design aids to help build microcomputer systems, so we do that. You can define as many businesses as there are companies in the business, because each has defined a different market that it's going after. Certainly IBM and DEC are both in the computer business, but you don't think of them as the same. There's a little segment where there's an area of competition, but in the main they're in different businesses. And I think that that's true here.

It's a good idea to know where your strength lies. Would you say that's one of the key things?

Yes, and certainly in strategic planning, the analysis of where our strengths and weaknesses lie is an essential part. We build on strength and try to stay out of competition where we're weak. Our strength is clearly in the components manufacture, in the design capabilities there, so that's where we want to compete. That's where we want to do battle with our competition. We certainly don't want to compete with IBM, anymore than we want to compete with General Motors. Just because we make an engine control, we don't want to make an automobile.

You don't want to be another IBM?

We'd like to be another IBM. I'd love to have 70% of the market. But getting into throwing rocks at each other is not nearly as productive as going on and building our own businesses.

When people like you and Kenneth Olsen and Edson deCastro, men who have been among the

prime movers in electronics, are gone, do you think Intel and DEC and Data General will be different?

Hewlett-Packard hasn't changed a great deal with the changing of the guard over there, and I think it's because it was a well-conceived, well-built organization. IBM hasn't changed a great deal since Tom Watson left. If you think of the character of IBM now compared to 20 years ago, it's a little different, but you can't say that there were any major changes in the thrust of the business. And again I think it's because it was a well-conceived, well-executed management style that works, so there was no need to change it.

Would Intel change, then, without you and Grove and Moore?

I believe that Intel has been a very successful company, that we have innovated in terms of how things are done, in terms of management styles, and in terms of culture as well as products; and I think the momentum is there that will keep it moving in that direction.

How would you say Intel differs from other companies in your industry?

I used to characterize our business as compared to others in the industry as working on the edge of disaster. We are absolutely trying to do those things which nobody else could do from a technical point of view. We measure everything that we do so that when something goes wrong we have some idea of what it was that went wrong—a very complex process. We've tried to extend that same philosophy to the running of the whole organization. You don't do something unless you know what you're doing. You don't change something unless you know that it's been done on a pilot basis, that it won't louse up something else. And our industry's unique in that because it is very, very complex in terms of the technology that goes into it.

And it's very easy to make a mistake?

Very, very easy to make a mistake. We're working where a speck of dust ruins everything—that kind of an environment as far as the actual production is concerned.

You probably couldn't start an Intel today, could you?

I think you could start an Intel. It wouldn't be in this field. I think that there are still plenty of opportunities.

But it would take a tremendous amount of money, wouldn't it?

This field would. But there are significant companies that were started with relatively little. One of my favorites is called Apple Computer. And the guy started it by selling a car, and that was the capital. He started it in his garage, literally.

And he and his partner were only in their twenties, too, weren't they?

That's right. So it's like the start-up of Hewlett-Packard, which was done in a garage with $5,000. That was a lot more money when Hewlett and Packard started than when these guys started recently on $5,000. So, we're talking about those opportunities that are brain-intensive rather than capital-intensive.

But mergers and acquisitions are still cutting down the number of companies. How long will Apple Computer or a company like that be what it is today?

I don't know. A similar question is whether the acquisitions of the semiconductor companies have really decreased the number of competitors or not. They're still in business. Fairchild is still selling whether it's part of

Schlumberger or not. Mostek will exist whether it's part of United Technologies Corporation or not. I was sad to see Fairchild merged quite as early as it was, in the sense that this last quarter we finally beat it in volume.

You weren't sad because of sentimental feeling about your beginnings there?

No. Just straight competition.

When you started Intel, did you have trouble getting capital?

No, we never really had any trouble getting money. It may shock a lot of people to find this out, but we never wrote a business plan, never wrote a prospectus. We just said, "We're going into business; would you like to support it?"

But you did have the experience and the expertise?

We had a track record. There was clearly a great demand for semiconductors. It was still a rapid growth environment during that time.

Howard Head once said that, when he started Head Ski, if there was a sales meeting to attend he'd attend it, if there was an ad to write he'd write it, if there was a floor to sweep he'd sweep it. That can be a problem for a lot of entrepreneurs. Did you ever have to do everything?

I've scrubbed the floors, I've done the glassblowing, I've run diffusion furnaces, and so on, in the past; I've done the customer calls and I've talked at sales meetings.

Did you ever feel that you had to?

No, those were the things to be done, so l did them. I guess if there is a frustration in a larger organization, it is that it takes longer to see the results of what you're doing. There's a massive inertia. So that you push on one thing and a year later you can see the movement. A small organization can turn on a dime and change direction. You suggest another way to do things and you can get it implemented in a week or two. When you have 10,000 people to change the direction of, it just doesn't happen that way. What you hope you do, or can do, is to break the organization down into small manageable units so that you can change the direction of one unit at a time. And I think that has been done effectively.

So being effective in the organization is the way you find a challenge?

There's an enormous satisfaction in seeing that you've really affected the society, and I have no doubt in my mind that Intel has really affected our society. If nothing else, the microcomputer revolution is an Intel-induced change that has occurred in our society. And we're just beginning to see some changes that are going on in the society because of it. It is much less necessary to be in the city for communicating now than it was 20 years ago. As a matter of fact, the necessity of going to work is much less now because you can have communication facilities at home so that you can work at home. We have several engineers who have their terminals at home. They can work just as well there as they can here.

In your role as vice-chairman, do you personally have more time to spend at home?

No. I intended to, but it doesn't work out that way.

How many hours a week do you work?

Oh, I usually get in here by 7:45 to 8:00 and usually go home about 6:00 or 6:30. I don't work weekends, at least not in the office.

Do you take work home with you?

Reading. There are such voluminous amounts to try to get through to keep up with what's going on. I am willing to take more vacation time than I used to be able to.

Were you able to before but you just wouldn't?

Precisely. And actually that is one of the reasons why Intel was a two-headed monster when we started it. In the Fairchild situation, I simply felt that I couldn't leave and relax, which is a stupid way to run your life. One of the primary objectives in getting Intel going was to have it arranged so that I could leave and relax, and I started out with a partner that I could trust, whose judgment I trusted. Beyond that the energy goes into organizational building and team building, so that the team can carry on the job.

Now that you've removed yourself more or less from day-to-day operations, do you miss that?

Yes. How should I put this? I wanted to remove myself from the day-to-day operations so there would be more time to think about some other things, but that's a difficult thing to do, too. Some of the time you wonder about what you are doing. I mean, the complexity of the organization is such that it's an absolutely full-time job just to keep up with what is going on. It's several full-time jobs, as a matter of fact.

So it becomes dangerous to try to do something else as well as be involved in daily operations, because you don't have enough knowledge about what's going on and you make some horrible mistakes. Too many people depend on you to be right to take that risk. If you're going to try to do other things beyond that, then you'd better be sure that somebody is watching the store. But it is so habitual to watch the store that it becomes somewhat of a role crisis doing something else. I think that there are broader issues, however, that need to be thought about anyway.

Do you mean that there are broader national issues that you'd like to think about?

Maybe that's the motivation. Where's American capitalism going? Is it going down the tubes or is it going to survive? Where is the American standard of living going? Is it going to bread and circuses as it has been for the last decade or is it going to do what we did in the 1960s, that is, continually increase the standard of living for the population? Where's our international competitive situation going? Are we going to have the discipline to solve the energy problem in the United States? It's those kinds of questions that I think are important.

What is your major concern right now?

My major concern right now for all U.S. business is how we are going to compete with Japan. Because they're doing it right, and we're doing it wrong.

Well, we must be doing some things right. You are; this industry is.

But if you look at what gave Americans strength, it was the high level of motivation in innovation, the high availability of venture capital; and you look at the industry now, it's capital intensive. Now suddenly you have a major shift in the advantages and disadvantages.

What can be done about it?

As a nation we can't let Japan win this competitive battle because of complacency. I think we're much more alert to the situation than the automobile industry was—or the steel industry, the TV industry, the tape recorder industry, the ball-bearing industry, the bicycle industry, or the motorcycle industry. Just list them all as they disappear out of American society because of Japan competition. It's a little frightening to think that this is happening in this industry right now. Yes, the semiconductor industry is healthy right now, but if we are to remain healthy, some changes will have to be made.

What kinds of changes are you thinking of?

In America, there's so little investment capital available that it's come to a situation where you pick the low hanging fruit and you don't worry about planting the new trees. You don't have the resources available to do both. And I think that's the thing that's likely to damage American industry. If there isn't a change in that, this industry, which is a centerpiece of American technology, could all be lost to the Japanese.

Reading 11

The Discipline
of Teams

By
Jon R. Katzenbach and Douglas K. Smith

Early in the 1980s, Bill Greenwood and a small band of rebel railroaders took on most of the top management of Burlington Northern and created a multibillion-dollar business in "piggybacking" rail services despite widespread resistance, even resentment, within the company. The Medical Products Group at Hewlett-Packard owes most of its leading performance to the remarkable efforts of Dean Morton, Lew Platt, Ben Holmes, Dick Alberting, and a handful of their colleagues who revitalized a health care business that most others had written off. At Knight-Ridder, Jim Batten's "customer obsession" vision took root at the *Tallahassee Democrat* when 14 frontline enthusiasts turned a charter to eliminate errors into a mission of major change and took the entire paper along with them.

Such are the stories and the work of teams—real teams that perform, not amorphous groups that we call teams because we think that the label is motivating and

Reprinted by permission of the *Harvard Business Review*, "The Discipline of Teams," (March-April, 1993). Copyright © 1993 by the President and Fellows of Harvard College; all rights reserved.

energizing. The difference between teams that perform and other groups that don't is a subject to which most of us pay far too little attention. Part of the problem is that team is a word and concept so familiar to everyone.

Or at least that's what we thought when we set out to do research for our book, *The Wisdom of Teams*. We wanted to discover what differentiates various levels of team performance, where and how teams work best, and what top management can do to enhance their effectiveness. We talked with hundreds of people on more than 50 different teams in 30 companies and beyond, from Motorola and Hewlett-Packard to Operation Desert Storm and the Girl Scouts.

We found that there is a basic discipline that makes teams work. We also found that teams and good performance are inseparable; you cannot have one without the other. But people use the word team so loosely that it gets in the way of learning and applying the discipline that leads to good performance. For managers to make better decisions about whether, when, or how to encourage and use teams, it is important to be more precise about what a team is and what it isn't.

Most executives advocate teamwork. And they should. Teamwork represents a set of values that encourage listening and responding constructively to views expressed by others, giving others the benefit of the doubt, providing support, and recognizing the interests and achievements of others. Such values help teams perform, and they also promote individual performance as well as the performance of an entire organization. But teamwork values by themselves are not exclusive to teams, nor are they enough to ensure team performance.

Nor is a team just any group working together. Committees, councils, and task forces are not necessarily teams. Groups do not become teams simply because that is what someone calls them. The entire work force of any large and complex organization is never a team, but think about how often that platitude is offered up.

To understand how teams deliver extra performance, we must distinguish between teams and other forms of working groups. That distinction turns on performance results. A working group's performance is a function of what its members do as individuals. A team's performance includes both individual results and what we call "collective work-products." A collective work-product is what two or more members must work on together, such as interviews, surveys, or experiments. Whatever it is, a collective work-product reflects the joint, real contribution of team members.

Working groups are both prevalent and effective in large organizations where individual accountability is most important. The best working groups come together to share information, perspectives, and insights; to make decisions that help each person do his or her job better; and to reinforce individual performance standards. But the focus is always on individual goals and accountabilities. Working group members don't take responsibility for results other than their own. Nor do they try to develop incremental performance contributions requiring the combined work of two or more members.

Teams differ fundamentally from working groups because they require both individual and mutual accountability. Teams rely on more than group discussion, debate, and decision; on more than sharing information and best practice performance standards. Teams produce discrete work-products through the joint contributions of their members. This is what makes possible performance levels greater than the sum of all the individual bests of team members. Simply stated, a team is more than the sum of its parts.

The first step in developing a disciplined approach to team management is to think about teams as discrete units of performance and not just as positive sets of values. Having observed and worked with scores of teams in action, both successes and failures, we offer the following. Think of it as a working definition or, better still, an essential discipline that real teams share.

A team is a small number of people with complementary skills who are committed to a common purpose, set of performance goals, and approach for which they hold themselves mutually accountable.

The essence of a team is common commitment. Without it, groups perform as individuals; with it, they become a powerful unit of collective performance. This kind of commitment requires a purpose in which team members can believe. Whether the purpose is to "transform the contributions of suppliers into the satisfaction of customers," to "make our company one we can be proud of again," or "to prove that all children can learn, " credible team purposes have an element related to winning, being first, revolutionizing, or being on the cutting edge.

Teams develop direction, momentum, and commitment by working to shape a meaningful purpose. Building ownership and commitment to team purpose, however, is not incompatible with taking initial direction from outside the team. The often asserted assumption that a team cannot "own" its purpose unless management leaves it alone actually confuses more potential teams than it helps. In fact, it is the exceptional case—for example, entrepreneurial situations—when a team creates a purpose entirely on its own.

Most successful teams shape their purposes in response to a demand or opportunity put in their path, usually by higher management. This helps teams get started by broadly framing the company's performance expectation. Management is responsible for clarifying the charter, rationale, and performance challenge for the team, but management must also leave enough flexibility for the team to develop commitment around its own spin on that purpose, set of specific goals, timing, and approach.

The best teams invest a tremendous amount of time and effort exploring, shaping, and agreeing on a purpose that belongs to them both collectively and individually. This "purposing" activity continues throughout the life of the team. In contrast, failed teams rarely develop a common purpose. For whatever reason—an insufficient focus on performance, lack of effort, poor leadership—they do not coalesce around a challenging aspiration.

The best teams also translate their common purpose into specific performance goals, such as reducing the reject rate from suppliers by 50% or increasing the math scores of graduates from 40% to 95%. Indeed, if a team fails to establish specific performance goals or if those goals do not relate directly to the team's overall purpose, team members become confused, pull apart, and revert to mediocre performance. By contrast, when purposes and goals build on one another and are combined with team commitment, they become a powerful engine of performance.

Transforming broad directives into specific and measurable performance goals is the surest first step for a team trying to shape a purpose meaningful to its members. Specific goals, such as getting a new product to market in less than half the normal time, responding to all customers within 24 hours, or achieving a zero-defect rate while simultaneously cutting costs by 40%, all provide firm footholds for teams. There are several reasons:

• Specific team performance goals help to define a set of work-products that are different both from an organization-wide mission and from individual job objectives. As a result, such work-products require the collective effort of team members to make something specific happen that, in and of itself, adds real value to results. By contrast, simply gathering from time to time to make decisions will not sustain team performance.

• The specificity of performance objectives facilitates clear communication and constructive conflict within the team. When a plant-level team, for example, sets a goal of reducing average machine changeover time to two hours, the clarity of the goal forces the team to concentrate on what it would take either to achieve or to reconsider the goal. When such goals are clear, discussions can focus on how to pursue them or whether to change them; when goals are ambiguous or nonexistent, such discussions are much less productive.

• The attainability of specific goals helps teams maintain their focus on getting results. A product development team at Eli Lilly's Peripheral Systems Division set definite yardsticks for the market introduction of an ultrasonic probe to help doctors locate deep veins and arteries. The probe had to have an audible signal through a specified depth of tissue, be capable of being manufactured at a rate of 100 per day, and have a unit cost less than a preestablished amount. Because the team could measure its progress against each of these specific objectives, the team knew throughout the development process where it stood. Either it had achieved its goals or not.

• As Outward Bound and other team-building programs illustrate, specific objectives have a leveling effect conducive to team behavior. When a small group of people challenge themselves to get over a wall or to reduce cycle time by 50%, their respective titles, perks, and other stripes fade into the background. The teams that succeed evaluate what and how each individual can best contribute to the team's goal and, more important, do so in terms of the performance objective itself rather than a person's status or personality.

- Specific goals allow a team to achieve small wins as it pursues its broader purpose. These small wins are invaluable to building commitment and overcoming the inevitable obstacles that get in the way of a long-term purpose. For example, the Knight Ridder team mentioned at the outset turned a narrow goal to eliminate errors into a compelling customer-service purpose.

- Performance goals are compelling. They are symbols of accomplishment that motivate and energize. They challenge the people on a team to commit themselves, as a team, to make a difference. Drama, urgency, and a healthy fear of failure combine to drive teams who have their collective eye on an attainable, but challenging, goal. Nobody but the team can make it happen. It is their challenge.

The combination of purpose and specific goals is essential to performance. Each depends on the other to remain relevant and vital. Clear performance goals help a team keep track of progress and hold itself accountable; the broader, even nobler, aspirations in a team's purpose supply both meaning and emotional energy.

Virtually all effective teams we have met, read or heard about, or been members of have ranged between 2 and 25 people. For example, the Burlington Northern "piggybacking" team had 7 members, the Knight-Ridder newspaper team, 14. The majority of them have numbered less than 10. Small size is admittedly more of a pragmatic guide than an absolute necessity for success. A large number of people, say 50 or more, can theoretically become a team. But groups of such size are more likely to break into subteams rather than function as a single unit.

Why? Large numbers of people have trouble interacting constructively as a group, much less doing real work together. Ten people are far more likely than fifty are to work through their individual, functional, and hierarchical differences toward a common plan and to hold themselves jointly accountable for the results.

Large groups also face logistical issues, such as finding enough physical space and time to meet. And they confront more complex constraints, like crowd or herd behaviors, which prevent the intense sharing of viewpoints needed to build a team. As a result, when they try to develop a common purpose, they usually produce only superficial "missions" and well-meaning intentions that cannot be translated into concrete objectives. They tend fairly quickly to reach a point when meetings become a chore, a clear sign that most of the people in the group are uncertain why they have gathered, beyond some notion of getting along better. Anyone who has been through one of these exercises knows how frustrating it can be. This kind of failure tends to foster cynicism, which gets in the way of future team efforts.

In addition to finding the right size, teams must develop the right mix of skills, that is, each of the complementary skills necessary to do the team's job. As obvious as it sounds, it is a common failing in potential teams. Skill requirements fall into three fairly self-evident categories:

Technical or functional expertise. It would make little sense for a group of doctors to litigate an employment discrimination case in a court of law. Yet teams of doctors and lawyers often try medical malpractice or personal injury cases. Similarly, product-development groups that include only marketers or engineers are less likely to succeed than those with the complementary skills of both.

Problem-solving and decision-making skills. Teams must be able to identify the problems and opportunities they face, evaluate the options they have for moving forward, and then make necessary trade-offs and decisions about how to proceed. Most teams need some members with these skills to begin with, although many will develop them best on the job.

Interpersonal skills. Common understanding and purpose cannot arise without effective communication and constructive conflict, which in turn depend on interpersonal skills. These include risk taking, helpful criticism, objectivity, active listening, giving the benefit of the doubt, and recognizing the interests and achievements of others.

Obviously, a team cannot get started without some minimum complement of skills, especially technical and functional ones. Still, think about how often you've been part of a team whose members were chosen primarily on the basis of personal compatibility or formal position in the organization, and in which the skill mix of its members wasn't given much thought.

It is equally common to overemphasize skills in team selection. Yet in all the successful teams we've encountered, not one had all the needed skills at the outset. The Burlington Northern team, for example, initially had no members who were skilled marketers despite the fact that their performance challenge was a marketing one. In fact, we discovered that teams are powerful vehicles for developing the skills needed to meet the team's performance challenge. Accordingly, team member selection ought to ride as much on skill potential as on skills already proven.

Effective teams develop strong commitment to a common approach, that is, to how they will work together to accomplish their purpose. Team members must agree on who will do particular jobs, how schedules will be set and adhered to, what skills need to be developed, how continuing membership in the team is to be earned, and how the group will make and modify decisions. This el-

ement of commitment is as important to team performance as is the team's commitment to its purpose and
goals.

Agreeing on the specifics of work and how they fit
together to integrate individual skills and advance team
performance lies at the heart of shaping a common approach. It is perhaps self-evident that an approach that
delegates all the real work to a few members (or staff
outsiders), and thus relies on reviews and meetings for
its only "work together" aspects, cannot sustain a real
team. Every member of a successful team does equiva-
lent amounts of real work; all members, including the
team leader, contribute in concrete ways to the team's
work-product. This is a very important element of the
emotional logic that drives team performance.

When individuals approach a team situation, especially in a business setting, each has preexisting job assignments as well as strengths and weaknesses reflecting
a variety of backgrounds, talents, personalities, and preju-
dices. Only through the mutual discovery and understanding of how to apply all its human resources to a common
purpose can a team develop and agree on the best approach
to achieve its goals. At the heart of such long and, at times,
difficult interactions lies a commitment-building process
in which the team candidly explores who is best suited to
each task as well as how individual roles will come together. In effect, the team establishes a social contract
among members that relates to their purpose and guides
and obligates how they must work together.

No group ever becomes a team until it can hold itself
accountable as a team. Like common purpose and approach, mutual accountability is a stiff test. Think, for
example, about the subtle but critical difference between
"the boss holds me accountable" and "we hold ourselves
accountable." The first case can lead to the second; but
without the second, there can be no team.

Companies like Hewlett-Packard and Motorola have an ingrained performance ethic that enables teams to form "organically" whenever there is a clear performance challenge requiring collective rather than individual effort. In these companies, the factor of mutual accountability is commonplace. "Being in the boat together" is how their performance game is played.

At its core, team accountability is about the sincere promises we make to ourselves and others, promises that underpin two critical aspects of effective teams: commitment and trust. Most of us enter a potential team situation cautiously because ingrained individualism and experience discourage us from putting our fates in the hands of others or accepting responsibility for others. Teams do not succeed by ignoring or wishing away such behavior.

Mutual accountability cannot be coerced any more than people can be made to trust one another. But when a team shares a common purpose, goals, and approach, mutual accountability grows as a natural counterpart. Accountability arises from and reinforces the time, energy, and action invested in figuring out what the team is trying to accomplish and how best to get it done.

When people work together toward a common objective, trust and commitment follow. Consequently, teams enjoying a strong common purpose and approach inevitably hold themselves responsible, both as individuals and as a team, for the team's performance. This sense of mutual accountability also produces the rich rewards of mutual achievement in which all members share. What we heard over and over from members of effective teams is that they found the experience energizing and motivating in ways that their "normal" jobs never could match.

On the other hand, groups established primarily for the sake of becoming a team or for job enhancement, communication, organizational effectiveness, or excellence rarely become effective teams, as demonstrated by the bad feelings left in many companies after experimenting with quality circles that never translated "quality" into specific goals. Only when appropriate performance goals are set does the process of discussing the goals and the approaches to them give team members a clearer and clearer choice: they can disagree with a goal and the path that the team selects and, in effect, opt out, or they can pitch in and become accountable with and to their teammates.

The discipline of teams we've outlined is critical to the success of all teams. Yet it is also useful to go one step further. Most teams can be classified in one of three ways: teams that recommend things, teams that make or do things, and teams that run things. In our experience, each type faces a characteristic set of challenges.

Teams that recommend things. These teams include task forces, project groups, and audit, quality, or safety groups asked to study and solve particular problems. Teams that recommend things almost always have predetermined completion dates. Two critical issues are unique to such teams: getting off to a fast and constructive start and dealing with the ultimate hand-off required to get recommendations implemented.

The key to the first issue lies in the clarity of the team's charter and the composition of its membership. In addition to wanting to know why and how their efforts are important, task forces need a clear definition of whom management expects to participate and the time commitment required. Management can help by ensuring that the team includes people with the skills and influence necessary for crafting practical recommendations that will carry weight throughout the organization. Moreover, management can help the team get the necessary cooperation by opening doors and dealing with political obstacles.

Missing the hand-off is almost always the problem that stymies teams that recommend things. To avoid this, the transfer of responsibility for recommendations to those who must implement them demands top management's time and attention. The more top managers assume that recommendations will "just happen," the less likely it is that they will. The more involvement task force members have in implementing their recommendations, the more likely they are to get implemented.

To the extent that people outside the task force will have to carry the ball, it is critical to involve them in the process early and often, certainly well before recommendations are finalized. Such involvement may take many forms, including participating in interviews, helping with analyses, contributing and critiquing ideas, and conducting experiments and trials. At a minimum, anyone responsible for implementation should receive a briefing on the task force's purpose, approach, and objectives at the beginning of the effort as well as regular reviews of progress.

Teams that make or do things. These teams include people at or near the front lines who are responsible for doing the basic manufacturing, development, operations, marketing, sales, service, and other value-adding activities of a business. With some exceptions, like new-product development or process design teams, teams that make or do things tend to have no set completion dates because their activities are ongoing.

In deciding where team performance might have the greatest impact, top management should concentrate on what we call the company's "critical delivery points, " that is, places in the organization where the cost and value of the company's products and services are most directly determined. Such critical delivery points might include where accounts get managed, customer service performed, products designed, and productivity determined. If performance at critical delivery points depends on combining multiple skills, perspectives, and judgments in real time, then the team option is the smartest one.

When an organization does require a significant number of teams at these points, the sheer challenge of maximizing the performance of so many groups will demand a carefully constructed and performance-focused set of management processes. The issue here for top management is how to build the necessary systems and process supports without falling into the trap of appearing to promote teams for their own sake.

The imperative here, returning to our earlier discussion of the basic discipline of teams, is a relentless focus on performance. If management fails to pay persistent attention to the link between teams and performance, the organization becomes convinced that "this year we are doing 'teams.'" Top management can help by instituting processes like pay schemes and training for teams responsive to their real time needs, but more than anything else, top management must make clear and compelling demands on the teams themselves and then pay constant attention to their progress with respect to both team basics and performance results. This means focusing on specific teams and specific performance challenges. Otherwise "performance," like "team," will become a cliche.

Teams that run things. Despite the fact that many leaders refer to the group reporting to them as a team, few groups really are. And groups that become real teams seldom think of themselves as a team because they are so focused on performance results. Yet the opportunity for such teams includes groups from the top of the enterprise down through the divisional or functional level.

Whether it is in charge of thousands of people or a handful, as long as the group oversees some business, ongoing program, or significant functional activity, it is a team that runs things.

The main issue these teams face is determining whether a real team approach is the right one. Many groups that run things can be more effective as working groups than as teams. The key judgment is whether the sum of individual bests will suffice for the performance challenge at hand or whether the group must deliver substantial incremental performance requiring real, joint work-products. Although the team option promises greater performance, it also brings more risk, and managers must be brutally honest in assessing the trade-offs.

Members may have to overcome a natural reluctance to trust their fate to others. The price of faking the team approach is high: at best, members get diverted from their individual goals, costs outweigh benefits, and people resent the imposition on their time and priorities; at worst, serious animosities develop that undercut even the potential personal bests of the working-group approach.

Working groups present fewer risks. Effective working groups need little time to shape their purpose since the leader usually establishes it. Meetings are run against well-prioritized agendas. And decisions are implemented through specific individual assignments and accountabilities. Most of the time, therefore, if performance aspirations can be met through individuals doing their respective jobs well, the working-group approach is more comfortable, less risky, and less disruptive than trying for more elusive team performance levels. Indeed, if there is no performance need for the team approach, efforts spent to improve the effectiveness of the working group make much more sense than floundering around trying to become a team.

Having said that, we believe the extra level of performance teams can achieve is becoming critical for a growing number of companies, especially as they move through major changes during which company performance depends on broad-based behavioral change. When top management uses teams to run things, it should make sure the team succeeds in identifying specific purposes and goals.

This is a second major issue for teams that run things. Too often, such teams confuse the broad mission of the total organization with the specific purpose of their small group at the top. The discipline of teams tells us that for a real team to form there must be a team purpose that is distinctive and specific to the small group and that requires its members to roll up their sleeves and accomplish something beyond individual end-products. If a group of managers looks only at the economic performance of the part of the organization it runs to assess overall effectiveness, the group will not have any team performance goals of its own.

While the basic discipline of teams does not differ for them, teams at the top are certainly the most difficult. The complexities of long-term challenges, heavy demands on executive time, and the deep-seated individualism of senior people conspire against teams at the top. At the same time, teams at the top are the most powerful. At first we thought such teams were nearly impossible. That is because we were looking at the teams as defined by the formal organizational structure, that is, the leader and all his or her direct reports equals the team. Then we discovered that real teams at the top were often smaller and less formalized—Whitehead and Weinberg at Goldman, Sachs; Hewlett and Packard at H-P; Krasnoff, Pall, and Hardy at Pall Corp; Kendall, Pearson, and Calloway at Pepsi; Haas and Haas at Levi Strauss; Batten and Ridder at Knight-Ridder. They were mostly twos and threes, with an occasional fourth.

Nonetheless, real teams at the top of large, complex organizations are still few and far between. Far too many groups at the top of large corporations needlessly constrain themselves from achieving real team levels of performance because they assume that all direct reports must be on the team; that team goals must be identical to corporate goals; that the team members' positions rather than skills determine their respective roles; that a team must be a team all the time; and that the team leader is above doing real work.

As understandable as these assumptions may be, most of them are unwarranted. They do not apply to the teams at the top we have observed, and when replaced with more realistic and flexible assumptions that permit the team discipline to be applied, real team performance at the top can and does occur. Moreover, as more and more companies are confronted with the need to manage major change across their organizations, we will see more real teams at the top.

We believe that teams will become the primary unit of performance in high-performance organizations. But that does not mean that teams will crowd out individual opportunity or formal hierarchy and process. Rather, teams will enhance existing structures without replacing them. A team opportunity exists anywhere hierarchy or organizational boundaries inhibit the skills and perspectives needed for optimal results. Thus, new-product innovation requires preserving functional excellence through structure while eradicating functional bias through teams. And frontline productivity requires preserving direction and guidance through hierarchy while drawing on energy and flexibility through self-managing teams.

We are convinced that every company faces specific performance challenges for which teams are the most practical and powerful vehicle at top management's disposal. The critical role for senior managers, therefore, is to worry about company performance and the kinds of teams that can deliver it. This means that top management must recognize a team's unique potential to deliver results, deploy teams strategically when they are the best tool for the job, and foster the basic discipline of teams that will make them effective. By doing so, top management creates the kind of environment that enables team as well as individual and organizational performance.

Reading III

Are You Walkin' What You're Talkin'?

By

Steven C. Brandt

"The last few people slip into their seats and a hush falls over the big room as the ceiling lights go dim. The CEO strolls to the podium, glances out at the sea of faces and begins: "Welcome to ...""

The annual calendar of almost every established organization is punctuated by one or more big, planned events. These events usually take the form of meetings for managers, sales people, or important customers. Many times these meetings are held away from the offices, labs, or factories. During such "offsites" the leaders often wear casual clothes as they mix with their assembled, similarly clad "troops."

Usually, there is both a formal and informal attempt to sell one theme or another to the eager participants. As mentioned in an earlier *Stanford Business School Magazine* article (December 1988), in recent years the themes for management meetings have tended toward subjects such as innovation, quality, competitiveness, putting the customer first, or becoming more global.

Reprinted with permission of *Stanford Business School Magazine.* © Steven C. Brandt 1990. All rights reserved.

Typically in these meetings, the importance of the people of the enterprise, particularly those in the audience, is stressed by the key speakers in connection with the theme. There may or may not be some break-out sessions to encourage the exchange of ideas. Then, after the CEO's closing remarks, the participants are released to return to their respective homes in the organization. Once there, however, it is not unusual for them to find in fairly short order, say within 90 days or so, that the reality of their day-to-day existence does not fit well with the rhetoric of the major event. Whatever the grand theme was, it turns out to have shallow roots, if any. The leadership of the enterprise isn't walkin' what it's talkin'.

For example, no amount of eyeball-to-eyeball cajoling at the offsite about the importance of customers will have much lasting impact if the managers of the enterprise get paid to produce sales volume at any cost. The finest fire-and-brimstone speech in the world on the merits of quality and its cousin, productivity, will dissipate unheeded by most of the attendees if the organization structure "back home" is unduly staff heavy and local success is based on making production quotas. The most dazzling, three-screen slide show ever created on the subject of teamwork or innovation (choose your topic) will have a half-life of two weeks if the dominant leadership style in the enterprise is an unpredictable mix of Pollyanna and Genghis Khan.

There are at least three unnecessary management problems that are created when important meetings are designed and conducted around content that is out of synch with on-the-job reality.

1. Money is wasted, particularly on offsite events.

2. Respect for the leadership is diminished to the extent that raised expectations go unfulfilled.

3. A fine opportunity to change or positively reinforce the existing corporate culture is lost by top management.

Money is wasted. When the hard and soft costs of taking from 25 to 250 people to a corporate watering hole for two to three days are totaled, it is a big number. In fact, a capital expenditure of the same magnitude would most likely have to go through all kinds of analysis before it would be approved. But typically, major events are not subjected to much scrutiny regarding the return they are to provide on the investment being made. Why not? There are several reasons.

First, major events tend to fall between the cracks in the organization structure. Who is in charge? Typically the answer is, no one. The date, agenda, and attendee list is a senior management committee product; the facility arrangements are done by someone with no budget or results responsibility; outside speakers are lined up by a person in Human Resources; and the actual flow of the meeting itself is designed by one or more people who have not done it before and who have no particular stake in any payoff.

Second, the desired results of the meeting are not pinpointed in advance. What are the participants to do differently because they attended? Are they there merely to hear or exchange ideas? Is the meeting somewhere in the Sunbelt really recognition of and a reward for those doing a good job? Or is the event supposed to cause people to do something different; e.g., to reallocate the way they spend their time, day-to-day? To paraphrase an old advertising axiom: "I know that half the money I spend on major events is wasted, but I don't know which half!" The primary cause is fuzzy objectives.

Third, a lot of money is wasted because the siting is overemphasized at the expense of the content; i.e., the icing is given more attention than the cake. I have seen more than one meeting in the last two years where the resources that were devoted to golf and celebrity speakers on irrelevant, unremembered (the next morning, even!) subjects were ten times the amount spent on the mainline, gut topics and experiences of the affair.

Respect for the leadership is diminished. In corporate life, the further a person is from key decisions and power, the harder it is to identify with the direction and spirit of the enterprise. The greater the distance from the center, the greater the centrifugal forces tugging on individual behavior patterns as they relate to customer service or quality, for example. Traditionally, as people were promoted, they spiraled upward and inward and became assimilated into the core group and its values. They became socialized or indoctrinated, in an anthropological sense. Now what happens when the promotion spiral essentially evaporates due to flattening, downsizing, and other corporate weight-loss maneuvers? What happens is that there is a void, or at least an unmet need, on the part of non-senior people for contact with those responsible for the health of the total enterprise, including the careers of those within. MBWA (Managing By Walking Around) helps a little as executives get out on occasion to chat and be seen, but MBWA doesn't penetrate far in companies of any size. Videotapes from the top are better than memos, but not a whole lot. It is mostly at the major events that key middle-level people get a chance to "touch" the top people.

When such an event is announced and a person is invited to attend, there are three levels of expectations formed. First, there is the expectation of exposure to the leaders. "I get to meet, talk with, and listen to some important people." Second, there is an expectation about the content. "I'm going to get high-level insights as to what is going on." And third, there is probably a mild expectation that things will be somewhat different after the get-together in ways related to the announced theme, whatever it is. To the extent that any of these expectations go unrealized, there is a cost in terms of post-event performance...and perhaps allegiance. This is particularly true in light of all the press today about the need for sound business thinking and execution in a turbulent world marketplace. When there is turbulence, both captain and crew need confidence in one another. In many ways, a major event exposes the leadership—for better or for worse. This may be why such events are frequently approached by senior people with trepidation instead of with an eye to the inherent possibilities.

An opportunity is lost. Like family birthday parties and holiday celebrations, major corporate events are perishable. The time for them comes and goes. If they happen, they immediately become history, once again, for better or for worse. Those responsible can't go back and redo or undo the occasion. I know of one management meeting that was allowed to degenerate into a full-blown gripe session, and there is still debilitating bitterness among the combatants two years later. And I am familiar with other events where the entire agenda was so tight and inflexible that the invited "participants" were mere spectators. The "shows" could have been staged much more cheaply on videotape and mailed out to the participants with equal impact. However, in my experience, most live events are neither particularly bad nor particularly good; they are, essentially, costly non-events. They are missed opportunities.

As with special family gatherings, important corporate meetings have the potential to hold or bring disparate organizational elements and individuals together around the campfire of shared experiences, ambitions, and plans. Each such event can be a positive, behavior influencing highpoint for the members of the gathered "tribe." Properly orchestrated or not, each such event is the occasion for ceremonies and ritual, the recognition of heroes and heroines, the giving of messages. The only issue is whether or not the net impact of the event–and all the events in the course of a year–carry the members of the tribe forward together in a desired direction; e.g., toward greater emphasis on the customer, higher quality work, more cost consciousness, profitable process innovation, etc.

Major live events also provide the designated leaders with their very best chances to listen (a great opportunity in itself) and to be seen and experienced "up close and personal." In most established companies, big management meetings provide the only occasions throughout the year when senior executives can display broadly some of the camaraderie, spirit, and cheerleading that is often an important part of their own success stories. And many students of managing believe that the regular display of such human characteristics is the only antidote to the institutional rigidity that is so much a part of our larger enterprises.

So, given the fact that there are so many management-type meetings, why is there a problem? Why is the experience curve flat? It is my view that the payoff is often less than it could be because 1) the events are thought of in tactical rather than strategic terms and 2) the seeds for follow-through by the participants are not planted in the preparation for and execution of the events themselves.

There are two actions to help correct these particular faults.

Plan and conduct major events to encourage specific behavior that supports the execution of the longer-range plans of the enterprise. It is useful to identify the main get-togethers already on the corporate calendar for the next two to three years. (If there aren't any, there probably should be if the enterprise has more than a few hundred employees.) Then, with an eye on the whole series, ask: How shall each event be shaped so that the cumulative effect of all of them contributes in a direct way to building—or maintaining—desired day-to-day performance, i.e., what people actually do? Major events modify the corporate culture, and culture, along with organization design and leadership style, drives behavior. And behavior is the track on which plan execution runs.

As you shape the events, there is one very common error to avoid. Do not have a different theme for each major meeting and, thereby, eliminate the opportunity for a cumulative effect. If a people-dependent topic such as quality manufacturing, customer orientation, productivity, or new product development is central to your way of competing in the 1990s, then that single theme bears repeating in lots of ways, over lots of days. If you decide that you do need multiple themes truly embedded in your enterprise, then develop a basic plan for all of your known events coming up over the next ten years.

Make each major event a pilot run on what the participants are to do when they return to their responsibilities. If you want more teamwork or more sharing of resources in the future, make sure that there are teamwork and sharing exercises in the meeting design. If quality is your message, then make it come alive via high-quality, high-participation experiences that sink the concept of quality work into the minds of the partici- pants. If listening and delegating enroute to greater empowerment is up top on your priority list for your management corps, and you really mean it, then survey i.e., listen, to the participants *before* the meeting and develop an agenda *with them* that responds to their con- cerns. If you want the customer to be number one, frame your major event around customer visits and testimoni- als, and demonstrate in vivid detail during the meeting just how customer "number oneness" will henceforth be measured and rewarded.

Major events are great opportunities. But to get a proper payoff, you have got to walk what you talk.

Videos by Author

MANAGING THE EMERGING COMPANY

- Ten-Subject Management Series
- 25-30 Minutes per Subject
- Each Subject Stands Alone
- Filled with Graphic Illustrations
- **Users Guide** for Each Subject

❏ STAGES OF GROWTH & KEY
MANAGING VARIABLES
   Stages of Growth
   Key Managing Variables
   The Big Picture
   (Item# MEC-001)

❏ BASIC PROFIT MECHANICS
   The Great Profit Myth
   Profit Mechanics
   How to Improve Profitability
   (Item# MEC-002)

❏ OPERATING ENVIRONMENT
& BASIC STRATEGIC PLANNING
   Factors
   Techniques
   Making Decisions
   (Item# MEC-003)

❏ SETTING EXPECTATIONS
   Expectations Pyramid
   Vision
   Mission
   Objectives
   (Item# MEC-004)

❏ STRATEGY
   Levels: Corporate; Business
   Vectors
   Developing a Sustainable
   Competitive Advantage
   (Item# MEC-005)

❏ ORGANIZATION DESIGN
   Historical Perspective
   New Rules
   Design Possibilities
   (Item# MEC-006)

❏ ORGANIZATION PROCESSES
   The Five P's
   A Business as a Brain
   Exploring Horizontal
   (Item# MEC-007)

❏ STYLE
   Three Kinds of Work
   Managing
   Leading
   (Item# MEC-008)

❏ PEOPLE
   How People are Alike
   How People Differ
   (Item# MEC-009)

❏ CULTURE
   Components of a Culture
   Examples
   (Item# MEC-010)

Videos available separately, or as a complete set.
For additional information, call **800-360-6166.**

Also by Steven C. Brandt

ENTREPRENEURING:

THE TEN COMMANDMENTS FOR BUILDING A GROWTH COMPANY

208 PAGES (ITEM# SCB-001)
ISBN 1-888925-02-7

$14.95

This hard hitting book presents ten proven operating principles for starting and building a successful company. With over 100,000 first  edition copies sold, noted entrepreneur and Stanford professor Steven C. Brandt offers updated guidance to entrepreneurs in the 90s.

- How to set objectives for yourself and the business
- How to select the right partners, investors, key employees
- How to define your product or service and market
- What to put in your business plan
- How to monitor and conserve cash and credit
- How to expand methodically
- How to avoid stress

This book covers key startup issues to help develop a solid foundation, including a guide to preparing an effective business plan. It details crucial operating matters and focuses on entrepreneurial professionalism. Written to be used, it is a proven tool spiced with 26 real-life case studies and charts, and anchored with the fundamentals for business success.

"A primer for entrepreneurs. I wish I had read this book years ago; it would have saved me a lot of trouble!"

-Bob Hannah, Founder, R.S. Hannah Co.

If you want to build a business, here is your handbook.

To order this new book, call **800-360-6166**, or complete the order on the last page.

How to order Books & Videos
from Archipelago Publishing

We hope you found *Focus Your Business* useful and helpful in building your business. If you have a business associate or relative who would benefit from having a copy of this book, here's how to order:

Single Copies
Please complete the ORDER FORM and mail or fax it to us. To order by phone, call toll free, 800-360-6166.

Quantity Orders
If you would like to distribute our books in your business or organization, or to your customers and clients as value-adding premiums, please call us immediately! Let us know how many copies you want, and we'll be happy to complete an order for you. We offer a substantial discount on orders of 25 or more books.

Archipelago Publishing
Build Your Business Guides
P.O. Box 1249
Friday Harbor, WA 98250
800-360-6166
Fax: 360-378-7097 • email: info@gmex.com

Build Your Business Guides & Newsletter
For more information about our *Build Your Business Guides* series, visit our website at **http://www.gmex.com**. There you will find excerpts from our books & videos, links to selected business resources, and other materials to help you build your business. Subscribe to our newsletter by completing the form on the last page of this book.

48° 44' 00"N
123° 15' 00"W
122° 44' 00"W
48° 24' 00"N

Archipelago Publishing
Friday Harbor, Washington

ORDER FORM

To order copies of this book or other business-building materials, complete this form and send or FAX it to:

Archipelago Publishing
Build Your Business Guides
P.O. Box 1249
Friday Harbor, WA 98250
FAX#360-378-7097

**ORDER BY PHONE
TOLL FREE!
800-360-6166**

Quantity Discounts Available

YES! Please send me the following books or videos:

Qty.	Title/Item#	Amount

TOTAL _____
(WA State Residents add 7.7% Sales Tax)_____
Shipping (see below)_____
TOTAL DUE:$_____

SHIP TO:

NAME:_____

ADDRESS:_____

CITY:_____ST:_____ ZIP:_____

DAYTIME PHONE:(   ) _____
(important)

Shipping Charges:
Book Rate: $2.00 for the first book and .75 for each additional book.
Priority Mail/First Class: $3.00 for up to three books.
Videos: $2.50 per video, or $15.00 for the series.

Payment:
Check Enclosed in the amount of $_____
Credit Card Orders: Visa or MasterCard Only

Card#_____ ex date:___/___

Signature:_____
Print Your Name:_____

For more information about any of our products & services, call
1-800-360-6166 or visit our website at http://www.gmex.com

**BUILD
YOUR
BUSINESS
GUIDES**

BUILD YOUR BUSINESS NEWSLETTER

Stay on Top! We'll keep you informed of new products, publications, and activities, along with seminar announcements and other valuable information that can help you build your business!

Please take a moment to send us your address, OR visit our website at **http://www.gmex.com** and complete the registration page.

YES! Please send me the Build Your Business Newsletter and put me on your mailing list!

Name:_____

Company:_____

Address:_____

City:_____St:_____Zip:_____

email:_____

Phone:_____

Fax:_____

Return this form to:
Build Your Business Newsletter
Archipelago Publishing
P.O. Box 1249
Friday Harbor, WA 98250

For immediate information about Build Your Business products and services, or to connect to our fax-on-demand service, call us at **800-360-6166**